THE SIHANOUKVILLE INQUIRY

A Play in Two acts

HL Serra

authorHOUSE®

AuthorHouse™
1663 Liberty Drive
Bloomington, IN 47403
www.authorhouse.com
Phone: 1-800-839-8640

First published by AuthorHouse 9/23/09

ISBN: 978-1-4490-1552-7 (sc)

Printed in the United States of America
Bloomington, Indiana

This book is printed on acid-free paper.

U.S. Sailing Directions

H.O Publication 161 (1970)

SIHANOUKVILLE (Kampong Saom)

10o 38′ N., 103o 30′ E.

World Port Index No. 57485

6.12- Sihanoukville is the principal port of Cambodia and the only port which can berth oceangoing vessels....

Landmarks: Two warehouses, easily identifiable from a distance, lie close S. of Pointe Loune, and nearly parallel to the main pier.

MAP OF SIHANOUKVILLE

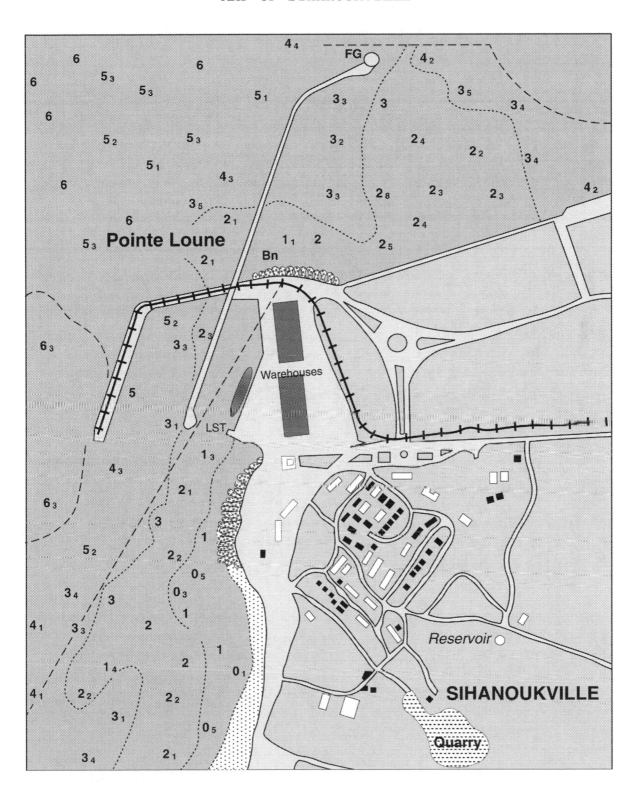

DESCRIPTION OF CHARACTERS:

(All dressed in tropical khaki navy uniforms except
MEDICI and METCALF who are in green, Vietnam-era
jungle fatigues, and YEOMAN who is in enlisted tropical
whites):

CARLSON:
Lieutenant-Commander, USN, 35, former Navy SEAL, wounded early
in VN war [slight limp], now navy Judge Advocate General [JAG]
Lawyer, designated to defend Lieutenant MEDICI. Loyal to SEALs—
Sea, Air, Land commandos— suspicious of MEDICI's motives and
judgments in the field. Above all, a careful lawyer dedicated
to his client's defense.

MEDICI:
Lieutenant, 23, USNR, NILO HA TIEN, [Naval Intelligence Liaison
Officer], black and blue spot with 2 inch cut scar on right
forehead, slight but fit, intense, sullen, nerves frayed by his
escapades in VN and Cambodia, and this board of inquiry. A
recent Princeton grad, he is sometimes ivy-league arrogant.
Enthusiastic, highly ambitious, the youngest full Lieutenant
in the Navy, he is becoming jangled from his activities in
Cambodia, for some of which he is being brought to inquiry.

BREUNER:
Lieutenant Colonel, 38, USMC, prosecuting JAG Corps officer for
Military Assistance Command Vietnam [MACV] in MEDICI's inquiry.
Perfectly uniformed and white-wall hair trim, not thread out
of place. Former Marine Corps reconnaissance commando veteran,
highly decorated, turned military lawyer. By-the-book, tightly
disciplined, company man. Humorless.

METCALF:
Gunnersmate First Class, 26, SEAL petty officer, on crutches
from gunshot wound to left leg, on special assignment to
MACSOG [Studies and Operations Group— covert assassination
and destruction operations] for the mission to Sihanoukville.
Very self-assured and certain about US and MACSOG's purpose in
Vietnam and Cambodia. Respectful demeanor, which barely covers
dislike for MEDICI, who wounded him, stopped his mission to
Sihanoukville, and ended his career as a SEAL.

O'NEILL

Lieutenant-Commander, USN, 45, commanding officer USS GARRISON COUNTY LST-972. Passed over for promotion, old for a LCDR, gray haired, and a real glad-hander company man, cover-his-butt kind of guy. Heavy Kennedy-Boston accent.

KELLY

Lieutenant [Junior grade], 22, USNR. Executive officer of SEAL Team One, DET Bravo. Very young and baby-faced— looks too young to be in military, he is trim, fit, sphinx-like when questioned about special ops.

BOARD MEMBER:

LARKIN:

Navy Captain, 42, gray hair, career JAG, Presiding Officer.

YEOMAN

Navy yeoman, 22.

THE SIHANOUKVILLE INQUIRY

SCENE: *Saigon, Vietnam. August, 1970, in the "Cambodian Shop" of U.S. Naval Intelligence, a single large room on the third floor of a former French colonial administration building adjacent to the French Embassy compound. Through the open double bank of windows (stage left) can be seen the French* tricouleur *flag on its pole at the embassy next door.*

The room is rectangular, twenty by forty feet. The door (stage right) into the room from the stairwell is a large, black steel plate with a heavy sliding bolt, and it clanks and slams heavily with a metallic ring whenever it is opened and closed.

The walls of the room are covered with blackboard size maps, framed with varnished wood, some covered in a light blue cloth, others with the cloth drawn back to reveal parts of Cambodia's coast and border with Vietnam, infiltration routes marked with thin red or blue tape lines. A six foot square enlargement of a chart on an easel behind the witness chair depicts the port facilities of Sihanoukville Cambodia, including the quai wall, basin, deepwater pier, and two warehouses (in red) at the junction of the quai wall and pier. It also shows the outline of a ship, the

*USS GARRISON COUNTY, alongside the
pier on the outside wall, near the
warehouses.*

*A single wood table covered in
green baize sits on a foot-high
platform centered upstage with a
chair behind it for the Board of
Inquiry officer, Larkin.*

*Downstage of this table, to
the left and right of it, are
two smaller rosewood tables
set at oblique angles to the
larger one, so audience can see
counsel, stage right table for the
Medici and Carlson, his defense
counsel, stage left table for the
prosecuting officer Breuner and
prosecuting witness Metcalf. In
corner, downstage left, is a small
table with red, secure military
telephone.*

*A hardwood witness chair with arms
and back of curving wood spokes
is on the platform center stage
and downstage of the big table.
The platform is new white pine,
obviously thrown quickly together
for the Inquiry.*

*A souvenir flag of Prince Sihanouk's
recently deposed Cambodian monarchy
hangs sloppily from one wall, next
to it a poster-sized photograph of
the smiling Prince, with a hand-
lettered sign under it saying "BYE-
BYE SNOOKIE. March 18, 1970"*

*Three tall four-drawer military
file cabinets with vertical steel
locking bars welded to the front
stand against the upstage right*

wall of the room just stage right of the black steel door. The cabinets bear large red and white diagonal striped posters with block letters announcing "SECRET, "TOP SECRET," and "SPECIAL COMPARTMENTALIZED INTELLIGENCE." A small wood table and chair sit in front of the cabinets, at which the Yeoman will sit tape recording the proceedings. A Casablanca ceiling fan turns slowly in the sweltering room.

Throughout the play random bursts of automatic weapons fire can be heard through the open windows.

ACT ONE

SCENE 1

OVERVOICE

By June of 1970, Cambodia's neutrality in the Vietnam war was over. General Lon Nol's [Lahn nole's] coup had ousted Prince Sihanouk [SEE-a-nook], Cambodia had joined US and South Vietnamese forces, and US troops had invaded the Cambodian border sanctuaries of the North Vietnamese Army, which in turn laid siege to the capital city of Phnom Penh [Nom-Pen], blockading the Mekong, the airport, and destroying the government's radio transmitter.

A single ship of the American Navy was sent to Sihanoukville [SEE-a-nook-vill], Cambodia's only deepwater port, on a secret mission to install a replacement transmitter for Lon Nol's [Lahn nole's] government. These events followed.

(*Lights up.*

SCENE: *Carlson, standing, leans forward, hands resting on the polished rosewood table, across which sits Medici, looking sheepish.*)

CARLSON
(*Menacingly*)
So the only person you've shot face-to-face in this war is Gunnersmate Metcalf, an American sailor!

(*Shakes his head.*)
Nice shootin', Tex!

(*Carlson stands up straight, intense*)

What disturbs me, Lieutenant, is this: Not only do you think you're smarter than these special warfare guys, but you seem firmly convinced you're morally superior to them. You don't dirty your hands with violent "wet" operations in Cambodia, but you go nuts when Metcalf tries to carry out HIS orders and destroy the warehouses at Sihanoukville [SEE-a-nook-vill]...

> (*Points at Medici with his forefinger on each "YOU"*)

...because no one informed YOU, and YOU disagreed with the idea.

> (*Carlson turns his back to Medici, with a slight limp steps away from the desk and stares through he window.*)

You knew exactly what you were doing when you went to Ha Tien [HAH-Tien] up on the border— two gold stripes and glory, and only an accidental chance of injury. You dash in and out of Cambodia, get shot at once in a while for credibility, publicize it all in your glib intelligence reports, and make yourself a hero. Low risk, high return.

> (*Carlson turns sharply to Medici, glaring with disdain.*)

Well sorry, Lieutenant. That's not what war's about. You're fighting a [dill-eh-tant] dilettante war, without getting your shoes dirty.

> (*Carlson picks up his briefcase and starts to walk out of the room. Says over his shoulder*)

Next time, Lieutenant, shoot the bad guys.

MEDICI
(*Medici jumps to his feet.*)
Does that mean you won't defend me in the inquiry?

CARLSON

(*Snorts*)
I think not.

MEDICI

(*Medici goes after Carlson, spins
him around by the shoulder*)

CARLSON

(*Carlson drops the briefcase,
braces as if to fight, then lowers
his arms to his side as Medici
retreats a half step.*)

MEDICI
Listen, Commander. Hear me out. You're not far wrong on my
motives for going to Ha Tien [HAH-Tien] in the first place. But
consider this: The job changes the man.

I was scared to death when I got there— thought I'd be shot
by a sniper as I jumped off the helo. But I got my bearings,
then realized that the only way I could do my job and get
intelligence was to cross the border into Cambodia and see
for myself. No one will write me orders to cross the border,
because it's illegal, so I just do it by hook and crook.

With sailors who park their junks on the riverbank and shop
in the market at the Cambodian village of Ton Hon. We walk
in and plant electronic sensors on the same paths the North
Vietnamese use at night to smuggle weapons across the border.

I cajole inexperienced helo pilots to fly a few kilometers
across the border to see what goes on in the North Vietnamese
ammo dumps, on the trails and the roads. I go up along the
coast in Cambodian ships, and in Vietnamese fishing junks
at night to see what I can of light signals between the gun
runners.

And when I can't get a ride, I just walk in, or get flown in
one way by my helo pilot buddies, so I can do reconn— alone,
with a lousy pistol tucked in my belt. My pal Frank Brown says
I'm the fucking Johnny Appleseed of Cambodia! Even the special

ops guys only go in under doctrine, with a trained squad of linguists carrying weapons and radios, and helos standing by.

CARLSON

(*Carlson, attentive, walks back to the table and leans against it.*)

Go on, Lieutenant.

MEDICI

I can't get any support or security, or even ask for it, because the whole damn mission is illegal. It violates international law, Cambodian neutrality, and our own Rules of Engagement!

(*Medici sits down, looking dejected.*)

It's my show and my risk all right— entirely mine. Staffers in Saigon won't look me in the eye when they tell me they can't help me if I continue my solo trips into Cambodia and get caught. Then they always wink and say, "But keep up the good work."

(*Medici shakes his head slowly, looking at the table top.*)

Do you know how isolated that makes me feel? I've got the enemy in front and this wishy-washy staff behind me. At least the special ops guys know their people will make an effort to rescue them if the squad's in trouble. I don't have shit to back me up. I AM my own security. Yet I keep doing it— because it's MY job.

CARLSON

(*Nods sympathetically.*)

MEDICI
(*Quietly*)
You're right. I don't get into firefights every day with platoons of North Vietnamese. It's not what I'm paid to do. But I never

13

know what's out there waiting for me. It's unimaginable risk each time I go, and my nerves show it. I haven't slept more than a few hours a night for months.

> (*Medici straightens up, meets Carlson's gaze, speaks with conviction and energy.*)

But damn it, Commander, I do it. I've made myself responsible for knowing what goes on in my part of Cambodia. And you've got to believe this: Metcalf had to be stopped from blowing the warehouses in Sihanoukville [SEE-a-nook-vill]. Their destruction would have been a disaster in every way. I'm sorry he was wounded, but he had to be stopped.

CARLSON
(*With hands in pockets, moves a few steps, then turns, with a flicker of a smile across his face.*)
You really go into Cambodia without support or security?

MEDICI
(*Nods once.*)

CARLSON
Lieutenant, you're a lot crazier than you look. I think you'll need help.

> (*Carlson picks up briefcase.*)

MEDICI
You'll defend me?

CARLSON
Yes... It's my job.

> (*Lights fade.*)

ACT ONE

SCENE 2

*(Lights up. Larkin, presiding
officer of the Board in tropical
khaki with ribbons is seated at
dais. Breuner sits with Metcalf at
one counsel table, Carlson with
Medici at the other. Breuner has
a file folder of naval messages
and a blue canvas Navy logbook in
front of him. Yeoman sits at small
table running tape recorder, and
escorting witnesses in and out of
room when they are called.)*

LARKIN

(Taps gavel)

This Board of Inquiry on matters occurring in Sihanoukville
[SEE-a-nook-vill] Cambodia on or about June 6, 1970 will come
to order. I apologize to counsel for the working conditions,
but due to the sensitive nature of these proceedings, and
the secrecy of this room itself, it was necessary to remove
the air conditioner to an Army repair shop rather than have
it repaired here by soldiers without the necessary security
clearances. You'll notice we have no reporter— we couldn't
find one with adequate security clearance— so the yeoman will
tape record the proceedings. You all are aware this room,
the Navy's Cambodian Intelligence Shop, formally does not
exist, but because of it's photo and map facilities relating
to Sihanoukville [SEE-a-nook-vill], and it's secret location,
it serves as an appropriate venue for these classified
proceedings. So bear with me and the heat, gentlemen.

Now, I understand this Board is to focus on events which
occurred during a naval mission to Sihanoukville [SEE-a-nook-
vill] during June 1970— about two months ago.

Colonel Breuner, is the judge advocate ready to proceed?

BREUNER

(Stands, remains standing)

15

BREUNER

Ready, your honor.

LARKIN

Commander Carlson, ready for Lieutenant Medici [MED-ih-chee]?

CARLSON

(*Stands*)

Ready, your honor.

(*Sits*)

BREUNER

May it please the court, on behalf of Commander, Military Assistance Command, Vietnam, I request this board at its conclusion to issue charges under the Uniform Code of Military Justice against Lieutenant Medici [MED-ih-chee], in summary:

1. For disobeying on June 6, 1970 LCDR O'Neill's direct order not to leave USS GARRISON COUNTY while in Sihanoukville, Cambodia;

2. For interfering on June 6, 1970 with the Studies and Operations Group— SOG's— direct orders to petty officer Metcalf to destroy two warehouses containing communist weapons at the port of Sihanoukville, Cambodia by physically injuring petty officer Metcalf by gunshot wound;

3. For disobeying on March 29, 1970 a direct Presidential Order not to supply weapons or ammunition to Cambodian forces...

CARLSON

Objection to the two June 6th specifications, your honor. First, under the definitions of SOPA [SOAP-uh]— senior officer present afloat— we believe that Lieutenant-Commander O'Neill was not Lieutenant Medici's [MED-ih-chee's] SOPA [SOAP-uh] on June 6th, and we move to strike that allegation.

Second, we move to strike the phrase "and physically injuring by gunshot wound." The court is aware there exist no assault

16

or battery charges in the UCMJ. If an enlisted man strikes an officer, it may be an Article 91 charge of Insubordinate Conduct. No similar charge exists if an officer strikes or injures an enlisted man.

LARKIN

(*Frowns, nods head.*)
On the SOPA [SOAP-uh] questions, I will consider those definitions as an affirmative defense during my deliberations. On the second point, counsel correctly states the code, and that portion of the specification which states "and physically injured by gunshot wound" will be stricken, leaving the requested charge of interfering with the execution of a lawful order.

But to forewarn you, Commander Carlson, I have decided to hear all testimony related to the shooting incident, so save your objections.

CARLSON
Then I will ask the Board to consider Article 91 insubordination charges against petty officer Metcalf arising from the same incident for assaulting Lieutenant Medici [MED-ih-chee], his senior officer present in the warehouse at Sihanoukville [see-a-nook-vill].

LARKIN
(*Testy*)
They will be considered. And you are pushing it, counsel.

(*Turns to Breuner*)

Any further charges you wish me to consider, Colonel?

BREUNER
Yes, your honor. The specifications relating to the delivery of American ammunition to the Cambodians on March 29, and interfering on June 6 with the destruction of the Sihanoukville [SEE-a-nook-vill] warehouses which contained tons of communist ammunition, each constitutes an Article 104 violation— aiding the enemy.

(*Medici and Carlson look at each
other, stunned; Larkin frowns, looks
at them, then back at Breuner*)

LARKIN

Any other charges the Judge Advocate wishes the Board to consider at conclusion?

BREUNER

Yes, your honor. One Article 88 charge— Contempt Toward Civil Officials— to wit, that on or about March 29, 1970, when warned that transferring American ammunition to Cambodian forces violated a direct Presidential Order, Lieutenant Medici [MED-ih-chee], serving as NILO Ha Tien [HAH-Tien], stated "Fuck Nixon and his Kraut."

(*Medici hides his eyes with his
hand, then turns to Carlson and
shrugs. Carlson stifles a smile,
shakes his head once*)

LARKIN

Any MORE charges, Colonel?

BREUNER

(*Shakes his head*)
No, your honor.

LARKIN

Very well. Call your first witness.

BREUNER

Lieutenant Commander O'Neill, commanding officer USS GARRISON COUNTY LST-972.

YEOMAN

(*Holds Bible, leads O'Neill to
stand*)

O'NEILL

(*Takes oath while standing*)

YEOMAN

Do you solemnly swear that the testimony you are about to give shall be the truth, the whole truth, and nothing but the truth, so help you God?

O'NEILL

I do.

(*Sits*)

BREUNER

Your full name and duty station, sir?

O'NEILL

Lieutenant-commander Robert J. O'Neill, commanding officer USS GARRISON COUNTY LST-972.

BREUNER

To what command was GARRISON COUNTY attached on June 6, 1970—about two months ago?

O'NEILL

We were attached temporary additional duty to Commander Naval Forces Vietnam on June 1, 1970, and taken away from our naval support activities in the western Pacific by special orders from CINCPACFLT [sink-pack-fleet].

BREUNER

What were those support duties?

O'NEILL

Carrying supplies from Guam to naval facilities in Saigon and Danang. The pre-emption orders forced us to change our scheduled return to Guam, transit the Saigon River to the Naval facility at Nha Be [Nah-Bay], pick up a ten kilowatt shortwave transmitter, barrage balloon, antenna and two navy technicians, and deliver them to Sihanoukville [SEE-a-nook-vill] Cambodia on June 6, 1970.

BREUNER

Did you know why?

O'NEILL

Well, not from the orders. But at Nha Be [Nah-Bay] the scuttlebutt was that the North Vietnamese Army had overrun the Lon Nol [Lahn Nole] government's Radio Phnom Penh [Nom-Pen] transmitter site in Cambodia, and knocked it off the air. Since we were new allies with the Cambodes from the time Lon Nol's [Lahn Nole's] coup [coo] deposed Prince Sihanouk [SEE-a-nook] in March, the transmitter we carried was to get the government radio back on the air to let the Cambodian people and foreign press know Lon Nol [Lahn Nole] was still in control. The transmitter had a long wire antenna held aloft by a big barrage balloon. Pretty clever set up, actually. Two enlisted technicians were sent along to install it and get it working during our 12 hours in Sihanoukville [SEE-a-nook-vill].

BREUNER
Was petty officer Metcalf one of the two enlisted technicians sent with the shortwave transmitter and listed on your orders?

O'NEILL
Yes.

BREUNER
Did GARRISON COUNTY take the transmitter and men to Sihanoukville [SEE-a-nook-vill]?

O'NEILL
Yes... Sihanoukville [SEE-a-nook-vill] is the only deepwater port in Cambodia. The Gulf of Thailand is very shallow— 60 feet at its deepest— and half the year the monsoon blows from the southwest with a long fetch up the Gulf which causes a huge swell, sometimes a twelve to 20 foot rise and fall against the quai [kway] wall at Sihanoukville [SEE-a-nook-vill]. My LST is shallow draft when unladen, so they figured I could get in, unload the transmitter easily enough even with the swell, and get out the same day. We didn't want any international incidents or embarrassing photos in TIME Magazine, what with all the political upset at home about invading Cambodia— Kent State and all. We heard the Cambodes had dredged a basin behind the seawall and we hoped it would provide an offloading site protected from the swell. Turns out we had to park outside the basin, near the warehouses.

(*Points off-handedly at the chart
behind him*)

BREUNER

Sounds pretty straight-forward a mission.

O'NEILL

That part was. Until the spook came aboard.

BREUNER

Are you referring to LIEUTENANT Medici [MED-ih-chee]? Naval
Intelligence Liaison Officer— NILO [NIGH-low] Ha Tien [HAH-Tien]?

O'NEILL

(*Sits up straight. Glares at Medici.*)
Yes, sir. On the way up the Gulf of Thailand we receive
this FLASH TOP SECRET message from Admiral Zumwalt ordering
GARRISON COUNTY to rendezvous at 0300 on June 4 with a
river patrol boat off Phu Quoc [Foo-Kwock] Island to embark
Lieutenant Medici [MED-ih-chee], NILO Ha Tien [HAH-Tien], for
transit to Sihanoukville [SEE-a-nook-vill].

BREUNER

For what purpose?

O'NEILL

Damned if I knew!

(*Larkin smiles*)

O'NEILL

His written orders, when he presented them, were James Bond
gobbledegook, ambiguous— go and come as he pleases; embark
and disembark when he wants; don't question him about his
activities— like that.

BREUNER

Did the orders pose a mission problem for you?

O'NEILL

Well, I was damned nervous about getting in and out of
Sihanoukville [SEE-a-nook-vill] without incident, toot sweet.
I didn't want some spook mucking it up. Everyone knows
Sihanoukville [SEE-a-nook-vill] was the main port for communist
weapons coming into Cambodia to be infiltrated across the
border into Vietnam. The press was watching it like a hawk,
and there had to be a lot of bad guys there. So I wanted this

to be a clean, in-and-out deal, with no complications. In at
first light, out before dusk.

BREUNER

Did LIEUTENANT Medici cause you any problems?

O'NEILL

You bet he did! From the get-go. We rendezvoused at three in
the morning in a driving monsoon with eighteen foot swells.
His patrol boat is bobbing like a cork, even loses a gunwale
rail scraping our side. Lieutenant Medici [MED-ih-chee] does
some acrobatics to get aboard. Someone drops his bag in the
Gulf and we have to fish it out in that foul weather. I'm on
the bridge and the NILO— that's what they call him— appears on
the bridge like a ghost and scares me half to death telling
me he's from naval intelligence. I'm thinking one of my men is
smuggling drugs or something.

And he was in U.S. jungle greens, but wearing this strange
Cambodian naval beret.

> *(sniffs)*

I thought it an affectation myself.

Then the NILO insists on waking my armorer at four in the
morning to get a gun cleaning kit and nine millimeter bullets,
'cause his *pistolo* got soaked in warm seawater. Then he stays
up, meticulously cleaning the pistol and camera gear. My
steward and armorer told me this.

CARLSON

> *(Carlson and Breuner jump each
> others lines re objections and
> response)*

Objection. Hearsay.

BREUNER

Reports received in the line of duty through the chain of
command by Captain O'Neill are not hearsay as to his state of

mind in which he gave the orders Lieutenant Medici [MED-ih-chee] violated.

LARKIN

Overruled. Continue, lieutenant commander.

O'NEILL

(*Agitated*)

Next morning the NILO briefs me and the Exec on <u>his</u> mission, which requires <u>my</u> ship and crew to do a port survey, locate buoys, piers, warehouses, and take soundings on the way into the harbor, since we've had no port information on Sihanoukville [see-a-nook-vill] for seven years. Suddenly our simple job got a lot more complicated.

(*Sits up straight. Regains composure.*)

But we didn't complain. Orders are orders, and the mission made sense.

BREUNER

Did Lieutenant Medici [MED-ih-chee] cause any discipline or order problems while on GARRISON COUNTY?

O'NEILL

Problems? You bet. The morning after he came aboard I was in my sea cabin and heard gunfire. I was about to send the ship to general quarters. We're fifty miles from Cambodia's coast. There's nothing on radar and the lookouts had reported no small boats nearby. I ran out to the bridge and there's the NILO on deck, shooting Pepsi cans off the tops of waves with his pistol. And on the bridge my Exec Mr. Poe's grinning like a cat, announcing over the ship's loudspeakers "Nice shootin', NILO." I'm furious because we have doctrine for the use of small arms aboard ship, and Lieutenant Medici [MED-ih-chee] doesn't ask, just starts shooting.

BREUNER

Okay, captain, but did this violate any order Lieutenant Medici [MED-ih-chee] was aware of?

O'NEILL

No. But it made me even more concerned that his mission in

23

Sihanoukville [SEE-a-nook-vill] was to shoot someone, which would cause a nasty incident, maybe get us detained there indefinitely, or my ship fired upon. I didn't like it. Don't forget, mission orders aside, my first responsibility is the safety of my ship and crew.

BREUNER

Did you ever ask Lieutenant Medici [MED-ih-chee] exactly what his mission was?

O'NEILL

No. He wasn't very approachable. He was very direct and businesslike— curt— around me. And I guess I really didn't want to know if he was up to no good. I just didn't want my ship hazarded or my crew harmed.

BREUNER

You didn't get along well with Lieutenant Medici [MED-ih-chee], did you?

O'NEILL

(*Embarrassed.*)

You could say that— but mission is mission, and I don't let things like personalities affect my orders.

BREUNER

Any other incidents before Sihanoukville [SEE-a-nook-vill]?

O'NEILL

The wardroom briefing. I asked Lieutenant Medici [MED-ih-chee] to brief my officers and me on the situation in Cambodia. Lieutenant Medici [MED-ih-chee] had spoken to Mr. Poe, and Mr. Poe informed me that Medici [MED-ih-chee] was sort of "Our Man in Cambodia," and very knowledgeable about what was going on.

(*Shakes his head*)

Boy, what a mistake letting him brief was!

BREUNER

Why?

O'NEILL

After dinner, I asked him to begin. He whips out this crazy-quilt map of Cambodia and puts it up on an easel. It's got

24

North Vietnamese Army and Khmer Rouge units identified in
grease pencil all over it, with reported troop strengths. I
mean, this was TOP SECRET stuff.

(*With excitement*)

To look at the map, you'd think Cambodia was being overrun by
North Vietnamese troops!

Then, Lieutenant Medici [MED-ih-chee] proceeds to tell us
Cambodia is quote "turning to shit" now that the North
Vietnamese are on the move because Lon Nol [Lahn Nole] joined
our side. And that Cambodia's future is quote "bleak and
possibly short." That's what he said!

MEDICI
(*Looks sideways at Carlson with a sheepish,
apologetic expression.*)

O'NEILL
Worst of all, he points out that units of the 9th North
Vietnamese Division— a heavy weapons division— have been
reported operating in the vicinity of Sihanoukville [SEE-a-
nook-vill]!

BREUNER
Did his briefing cause you a mission problem?

O'NEILL
No. A morale problem.

(*Shifts in chair*)
I was sure my young officers were upset and nervous at the
prospect of encountering an enemy heavy weapons division
in what was supposed to be a cake walk. I didn't want them
jittery when we entered Sihanoukville [SEE-a-nook-vill] the
next morning— the first American ship there in years.

BREUNER
What did you do?

O'NEILL
I pulled Lieutenant Medici's [MED-ih-chee's] map off the easel,
told him that was enough briefing, and left the wardroom.

BREUNER

Any other incidents?

O'NEILL

Finally, when we made Sihanoukville [SEE-a-nook-vill] and were alongside the quai [kway] wall, I asked Lieutenant Medici [MED-ih-chee] to join me to greet our official guests who came to receive the transmitter. The Cambodian Chief of Naval Operations, and our new American naval attache from Phnom Penh [Nom-Pen], who'd only been in-country a few days. Lieutenant Medici [MED-ih-chee] tells me he can't participate, because he is here without permission of our diplomatic mission, and it would be impossible to explain his presence. So he sat forward out of sight as the dignitaries came aboard, then snuck off the ship for whatever spook stuff he was up to. In violation of my first order to him.

BREUNER

What was that?

O'NEILL

I told him I didn't think he should go ashore in Sihanoukville [SEE-a-nook-vill].

BREUNER

Was that an order?

O'NEILL

On my ship, when I tell an officer I THINK he shouldn't do something— that's an order!

BREUNER

What did Lieutenant Medici [MED-ih-chee] say?

O'NEILL

He told me I had a copy of his written orders from Admiral Zumwalt, that to stay aboard would prevent his mission, and that he was going ashore. Then he tells me "Don't wait up for me, Captain. I can get back on my own. If I'm not here by 1700, just get underway without me." And he left the ship as I've described.

BREUNER

But he did return to the ship, didn't he?

26

O'NEILL

He did, I'm informed, about 1630 in the afternoon. I left
explicit orders with the officer of the deck, that if Lieutenant
Medici [MED-ih-chee] returned, he was to be kept aboard.
Period. No ifs, ands, or buts. The O-O-D said Lieutenant Medici
[MED-ih-chee] appeared agitated when he came aboard, and asked
him to keep an eye on petty officer Metcalf who was down at the
end of the pier. Lieutenant Medici [MED-ih-chee] darted below
and came back on deck with his pistol tucked in his belt. He
asked where Metcalf had gone, and the O-O-D told him Metcalf
had carried some seabags into the closest warehouse. The O-O-D
insisted that Lieutenant Medici [MED-ih-chee] stay aboard on
my orders, but Lieutenant Medici [MED-ih-chee] ran past him,
slid down the jacob's ladder, walked quickly to the warehouse
and went inside. I was called by the O-O-D and was on deck by
then, and I sent Lieutenant jaygee Poe and some armed men to
the warehouse to bring Lieutenant Medici [MED-ih-chee] back
aboard. Just after Mr. Poe disappeared into the warehouse, I
heard a single gunshot, and Mr. Poe came out and called for
our ship's medic to treat Metcalf. I was furious, but anxious
to get underway before dark. After he was given first aid, my
men carried Metcalf back aboard, and I put Lieutenant Medici
[MED-ih-chee] in hack— he could not leave his stateroom— for
the trip back to Saigon. Petty officer Metcalf was MEDEVACed to
hospital by helo, and I personally escorted Lieutenant Medici
[MED-ih-chee] back to Naval headquarters in Saigon, and tried
to file charges against him on the spot, but had to settle for
this board of inquiry.

BREUNER

Am I correct that the Article 92 charges you wish the Board
to consider arise specifically from Lieutenant Medici's [MED-ih-
chee's] failure to obey your order not leave GARRISON COUNTY
while in Sihanoukville [SEE-a-nook-vill]?

O'NEILL

Yes, but more specifically the second unequivocal order not to
leave the ship after he returned around 1630. If Lieutenant
Medici [MED-ih-chee] hadn't gone ashore to snoop Metcalf, none
of this would have happened...
(_points to Metcalf_)
And this young sailor would not have been severely wounded
trying to carry out his orders.

BREUNER

I have no further questions of this witness, your honor.

LARKIN

Cross-examination, Commander Carlson?

CARLSON

(*stands*)
Just briefly your honor. Lieutenant-Commander O'Neill, if Lieutenant Medici [MED-ih-chee] hadn't gone ashore and stopped Metcalf, the warehouses and much of the pier at Sihanoukville [SEE-a-nook-vill] would have been destroyed, wouldn't they?

O'NEILL

I suppose so. I have since learned their destruction was petty officer Metcalf's undisclosed mission.

CARLSON

Might that event have hazarded GARRISON COUNTY and its crew?

O'NEILL

Well, Metcalf said he set the timer to blow the warehouses after we were underway, so I don't think there could have been any real hazard...

CARLSON

Do you know for sure? Have you investigated how much ordnance was in the warehouse, how big the explosion would be, how reliable the timer was, and how long Metcalf set it for?

O'NEILL

Well, no... I don't know for sure.

CARLSON

Take a look at the exhibit, lieutenant-commander. Your ship was pretty close to those warehouses, wasn't it?

O'NEILL

(*Looks at chart exhibit, waffles*)
Well... perhaps it's not to scale...

CARLSON

But you are still sure "None of this would have happened" if Lieutenant Medici [MED-ih-chee] had stayed aboard at 1630?

28

O'NEILL

Yes, I'm certain.

CARLSON

Just a couple more things: Did Lieutenant Medici's [MED-ih-chee's] briefing make your young officers or YOU nervous about the North Vietnamese units around Sihanoukville [SEE-a-nook-vill]?

O'NEILL

(*Sputtering*)
Why, what do you mean "Make me nervous?" I've...

BREUNER

Objection, your honor. Argumentative and badgering the witness!

LARKIN

Sustained.

CARLSON

Withdrawn. Commander, did you know Lieutenant Medici [MED-ih-chee] is the youngest full Lieutenant in the Navy?

O'NEILL

I may have heard something like that from Mr. Poe. He and Medici [MED-ih-chee] were chummy.

CARLSON

Did Lieutenant Medici [MED-ih-chee] irritate you because he was a brash, highly competent up-and-comer, and you had already been passed over for commander?

O'NEILL

(*Astonished, livid*)

BREUNER

OBJECTION, your honor, this is irrelevant, argumentative and badgering to Lieutenant-Commander O'Neill.

LARKIN

(*Sharply*)
I agree, Colonel. Commander Carlson, I'm instructing you to

treat this witness with the respect due a naval officer.

CARLSON

Aye-aye, Captain. I'd like to reserve the right to recall this witness later.

LARKIN

(*Still mad*)
Very well. This witness is excused.

(*O'Neill leaves stand*)

LARKIN

Colonel Breuner, call your next witness.

BREUNER

Gunnersmate Second Class Richard Metcalf.

METCALF

(*Hobbles to stand on crutches, sits*)

YEOMAN

(*Holds out Bible*)
Do you solemnly swear to tell the truth, the whole truth, and nothing but the truth, so help you God?

METCALF

I do.

BREUNER

Please state your full name and duty station.

METCALF

Gunnersmate Second Class Richard Metcalf, 057-22-0555, United States Navy.

BREUNER

Petty officer Metcalf, what is your present command?

METCALF

SEAL Team One, CTF 77.7.9.1, DET [dett] Bravo. Attached temporary additional duty to Naval Special Warfare Group, Commander Naval Forces Vietnam, at Nha Be [Nah-Bay].

30

BREUNER

Who do you work for?

METCALF

That depends—

(*Grins nervously*)

We are attached directly to Admiral Zumwalt's Staff, but our missions can be assigned from a variety of sources through our task force commander, the SEAL boss at Nha Be [Nah-Bay].

BREUNER

How did you come to be on USS GARRISON COUNTY on June 5th and 6th, 1970?

METCALF

Two men from our Detachment were selected to assist setting up a new shortwave transmitter for the Lon Nol [Lahn Nole] government in Cambodia, our new—

(*Metcalf smirks*)

"ally."

METCALF

The North Vietnamese units around the Cambodian capital had blown up the main transmitter of Radio Phnom Penh [Nom-Pen]— knocked it off the air— when they surrounded Phnom Penh [Nom-Pen]. Our job was to set up a portable shortwave transmitter, generator and antenna at the port of Sihanoukville [SEE-a-nook-vill] so the Lon Nol [Lahn Nole] guys could broadcast their daily propaganda to the people of Cambodia AND the foreign press. To let everyone know Lon Nol [Lahn Nole] was still in control despite the strangle hold the North Vietnamese Army had on his feeble government.

BREUNER

You are quite knowledgeable about politics and the military situation in Cambodia—

METCALF

That's one of my jobs— political officer for DET [dett] Bravo. I'm supposed to keep up on military and political developments

31

in any area in which we operate.

                              BREUNER

How do you do that?

                              METCALF

Well, I read all the Army and Navy message traffic dealing with
action reports, political reports and intelligence reports.
I also get translations of broadcasts from enemy propaganda
radio in the area.

                              BREUNER
                    (*Looks askance at Medici*)
Sounds like you are thoroughly prepared for YOUR job, petty
officer Metcalf. By the way, what is your job?

                              METCALF

I am weapons and explosives specialist for DET [dett] Bravo.

                              BREUNER

Did you receive specialized training in these areas?

                              METCALF

Yes. Navy B School for weapons, and I am EOD qualified—
Explosive Ordinance Disposal— I can handle all types of
explosives.

                              BREUNER

Any other training?

                              METCALF
          (*Looks at Breuner with surprise for an instant, then
               continues, a little cocky*)
Of course. All SEALs are UDT-qualified before SEAL training.
We go through an arduous training period of eighteen months
at the Amphib Base in Coronado. Physical training, weapons
specialist training, language training, political training,
direct action training...like that!

                              BREUNER
          (*Paces behind counsel table, then stops and focuses
               intently on Metcalf, lowering his voice— serious*)
Was there a second part to your mission to Sihanoukville [SEE-
a-nook-vill]?

METCALF

Yes, sir.

BREUNER

What was that?

METCALF

(*Looks at Medici with disapproval*)
To destroy the two warehouses at the foot of the pier—
(*Points with one crutch at warehouses in red on the
large map of the port on the easel behind him*)
— if they contained communist weapons. That's exactly what
Lieutenant Kelly told me during the mission briefing.

BREUNER

How were you to accomplish this part of your mission?

METCALF

First, I had to be sure the weapons were in there. And they
were. I peeked through holes in the metal buildings on our way
out to deliver the transmitter gear in the morning—

BREUNER

Of June sixth?

METCALF

of June sixth— and saw rows of crates of Russian and Chinese
weapons in both buildings.

We had to hustle to get the long wire antenna and generator
set up during daylight, and we accomplished it because we had
rehearsed it several times in Nha Be [Nah-Bay]. I alone was
assigned the warehouse mission, so I had to deal with it AFTER
we set up the transmitter. We finished with the set up around
1500, and I asked the Cambodes to drive us back to the ship
since we were to get underway as soon as we completed the
installation.

I had left all my explosives gear in locked seabags at the
guard shack on the pier, telling them it was stuff for the
transmitter. After we returned to GARRISON COUNTY the Cambode
guards left, and I quietly entered warehouse one—

33

> (*points with crutch to it on harbor map—*
> *closest to GARRISON COUNTY*)

— and carried my explosives gear inside— it was heavy with the
nitrogen bottles and all.

BREUNER

Nitrogen?

METCALF

Yes. It was a "N-E-W"— nitrogen enhanced weapon, that the
Teams had experimented with at Dam [damn] Neck, Virginia. If
you detonate regular C-4 plastique in a nitrogen-enhanced
environment, you get an explosion about 10-15 times more
powerful. For field use, all we had to do was make a teepee
with a couple of ponchos, set the C-4 charges inside it with
nitrogen gas saturating the interior of the teepee— then BOOM—

> (*Laughs nervously*)

— Bye-bye warehouses and weapons.

BREUNER

How far did you get before Lieutenant Medici [MED-ih-chee]
interfered?

CARLSON

Objection— leading. Calls for a legal conclusion that
Lieutenant Medici [MED-ih-chee] "interfered"...

LARKIN

Sustained. Colonel, please keep to the facts, I'll draw the
conclusions.

BREUNER

Certainly, your honor.

> (*to Metcalf*)

Did you install the explosives inside the warehouse?

METCALF

Yes. I got into the first warehouse by breaking the hasp. I
carried the seabags to the middle of the warehouse— in the

middle of the weapons crates— and proceeded to build a hollow
pyramid with crates of artillery shells. I stripped the C-4
plastique explosive bars, set detonation cord around them,
and connected them all to the timer wire. Then I wrapped the
pyramid of crates with the ponchos, sealed them good and tight
and taped the seams. I opened the nitrogen tanks to ooze gas
into the teepee nice and slow. There was plenty of gas to keep
it saturated for awhile, while the timer was running.

                    BREUNER
Then what happened?

                    METCALF
I was setting the timer, when I hear from behind me someone
say in a pretty high voice "What the hell are you doing?"

                    BREUNER
Who said that?

                    METCALF
I turned my head slowly and saw-

          (*points to Medici, voice rises*)

THAT Lieutenant pointing a pistol at me!

                    BREUNER
Were you surprised?

                    METCALF
I was shocked! First, all I could think was that the Cambodes
had caught me— then I couldn't believe one of my own navy guys
was pointing a weapon at me!

                    BREUNER
Then what happened?

                    METCALF
He starts some kind of discourse with me about "What am I
doing? Why blow the warehouses? No one told HIM what the plan
was," like that. Then he says something about the White House
sending 2,000 rifles to Cambodia, why would they want to blow
up these warehouses now that we were on the same side?

35

BREUNER

What did you do?

METCALF

The lieutenant was obviously confused— and un-informed. I told him the mission was authorized by the Studies and Observations Group— SOG. That's all I could say, I was so astonished. Then he looked really confused.

BREUNER

What happened next?

METCALF

He told me to cut the wire.

BREUNER

From the timer to the explosives?

METCALF

Yes. Then he screamed "Cut the fucking wire now!"

BREUNER

What did you do?

METCALF
(*Sits up straight in the chair, very formal*)
I determined that Lieutenant Medici [MED-ih-chee] was confused, an impediment to my mission, and had to be dealt with.

BREUNER

How did you do that?

METCALF
(*Clears his throat*)
I was kneeling on one knee. I nodded twice to him, as if to say 'OK', and unsheathed my K-Bar knife as if to cut the timer wire. Then there was shouting from the end of the warehouse. Lieutenant Medici [MED-ih-chee] was distracted, so I hurled my K-Bar at him. It hit his forehead, and he fell. As I leapt to disarm him, he discharged the pistol—

(*Squirms in his chair and looks disdainfully
at Medici*)

36

— and by dumb luck hit me in the leg. I was on him where he had fallen to the floor. Next thing I know the ship's exec, Lieutenant Jaygee Poe, and several armed sailors are pulling us apart, calling for the medic and carrying me out— I lost a lot of blood.

BREUNER

Were the warehouses destroyed?

METCALF

(*Lowers his eyes*)

No. The ship's armorer told me he disarmed the explosives, disassembled the whole thing, re-stacked the cases of artillery shells, and threw all the C-4 and nitrogen bottles off the pier. Kinda cleaned up after me.

BREUNER

Do you believe Lieutenant Medici [MED-ih-chee] physically interfered with your carrying out your lawful orders?

CARLSON

Objection— leading, calls for a legal conclusion.

LARKIN

Sustained.

BREUNER

Do you believe Lieutenant Medici [MED-ih-chee] interfered with your mission to destroy the warehouses?

METCALF

Yes. He screwed the whole deal up.

BREUNER

To your knowledge, did your inability to carry out your mission orders result in any aid or benefit to North Vietnamese forces in Cambodia?

METCALF

I believe so, sir. We have received reports that weapons from the warehouse were removed at night by trucks in the two weeks following June 6th to undisclosed locations in the vicinity of the Cambodia-Vietnam border. Presumably for infiltration into Vietnam, or use by North Vietnamese forces along the border.

CARLSON

Objection: "Presumably" and what follows are pure speculation.
Move to strike.

LARKIN

Sustained and stricken.

BREUNER

Nothing further, your honor.

LARKIN

Cross-examination, Commander Carlson?

CARLSON

Yes, your honor.

(*Walks slowly to within a few feet of Metcalf*)

Petty officer Metcalf, do you speak or read French?

METCALF

No, sir.

CARLSON

Khmer? [Kuh-mair]

METCALF

No, sir.

CARLSON

Vietnamese?

METCALF

Yes, sir. Southern dialect.

CARLSON

Were you sent to school to learn Vietnamese?

METCALF

Yes, sir. Monterrey Defense Language Institute for a year.

CARLSON

Did they also teach Khmer[Kuh-mair] there, if you know?

METCALF

I don't think they did, sir. I understand it's mostly a spoken language and not completely written the way Vietnamese is.

CARLSON

Not written into transliterated English characters, like Vietnamese is?

METCALF

I'm not completely sure, sir, but I think it's in Sanskrit type characters.

CARLSON

Very good— it is Sanskrit-based.

BREUNER

(*Stands*)

Objection, your honor. This entire line of questioning is irrelevant to the events of June sixth.

LARKIN

Response, commander?

CARLSON

If the court will indulge me, it is very relevant to Gunnersmate Metcalf's understanding of events in Cambodia on that day, and the soundness of his orders when countermanded by a senior officer present, Lieutenant Medici [MED-ih-chee].

LARKIN

Very well, proceed.

CARLSON

Petty officer Metcalf, can someone trained in Vietnamese understand spoken Khmer?

METCALF

Generally not, sir. The languages come from different cultural and ethnic bases.

CARLSON

What languages did your Cambodian navy and army contacts speak in Sihanoukville [SEE-a-nook-vill]?

39

METCALF

Khmer or French to each other, a tiny bit of Vietnamese, and pidgin English to us.

CARLSON

Do you know why they speak French?

METCALF

I believe because all their formal military training was done by the French, in Cambodia and at the French naval and military academies, right up through the 1960s.

CARLSON

You spoke of reading action, political and intelligence reports from army and navy traffic, and broadcasts of enemy propaganda in the area—

METCALF

Yes, sir—

CARLSON

Any of those reports in Khmer [Kuh-mair], French or Vietnamese?

METCALF

No, sir. They're all in English.

CARLSON

I meant the sources— any of the sources from Khmer [Kuh-mair], French or Vietnamese language reports?

METCALF
(*Hesitates*)
Well I assume some must be, where else would they get that stuff?

CARLSON

Who is "they" Metcalf?

METCALF

Well, the intelligence reporters.

CARLSON

Do you know who these reporters are? Explicitly what their sources are?

METCALF

Well, no sir, they are just reported on the daily message traffic boards. But I do know when we do missions in Vietnam there are generally identified sources from our military intel networks.

CARLSON

From NILOs around Vietnam?

METCALF

In the case of navy intel, yes. For the army it's from the 5-2-5 Military Intelligence Group and Special Forces Teams in the field— generally tactical stuff— unit locations, weapons, maybe reporting the general mission objectives of the units.

CARLSON

Do you regularly review any CIA information or reports in keeping yourself informed?

METCALF

No. That's civilian authority under the U.S. Embassy's control. I'm sure they communicate daily with the military intelligence guys.

CARLSON

Do you know as a fact they do that?

METCALF

Not as a fact, no sir.

CARLSON

Are you sure you were as well informed as you could be about conditions in Cambodia during your June 6, 1970 mission?

METCALF
            (*Authoritatively*)
YES SIR.

CARLSON

What were the enemy units around Sihanoukville [SEE-a-nook-vill] on June sixth?

METCALF

Probably small VC or KR units under cover in town— not

enough to pose a serious threat to our mission to set up the shortwave transmitter.

                              CARLSON

Probably?

                              METCALF

I was sure enough to require only our own personal weapons and a small Cambodian Army unit for our physical security.

                              CARLSON

How about pier and port security for the ship?

                              METCALF

Commander O'Neill was concerned about his ship, as he should be, but we knew the piers were guarded lightly during the day, and usually not at all at night.

                              CARLSON

From what source?

                              METCALF

Navy intel.

                              CARLSON

From NILO Ha Tien [HAH-Tien]— Lieutenant Medici's [MED-ih-chee's] reports?

                              METCALF
                    (Caught unaware)
Including NILO reports— yes. I don't know if they were NILO Ha Tien [HAH-Tien]— LIEUTENANT Medici's [MED-ih-chee's] reports or not.

                              CARLSON

But you can't say they weren't, correct?

                              METCALF

Correct.

                              CARLSON

What did you know about the political situation in Cambodia on June sixth?

METCALF

Well, as I said before, I knew the General Lon Nol [Lahn Nole] government was reportedly on our side after the overthrow of Prince Sihanouk [SEE-a-nook] in March. They were our allies for the moment.

CARLSON

Did you think that alliance might change?

METCALF

Of course! I think it was Henry Kissinger who called Cambodia a third-rate, piss-ant country that wasn't going to dictate foreign policy to the U.S. SOG thought Lon Nol [Lahn Nole] could fall any day. We knew there were North Vietnamese Army heavy weapons units holding the capital, Phnom Penh [Nom-Pen], under siege— that's why they needed the alternate transmitter site in Sihanoukville [SEE-a-nook-vill]. You wouldn't know day to day what would happen in Cambodia.

CARLSON

Is that how the decision was made by SOG to destroy the warehouses at Sihanoukville [SEE-a-nook-vill]?

METCALF

The decision? I'm not sure about how the decision was made, I just follow my orders.

CARLSON

Orders from whom?

METCALF

Like I said before...

(*Shifts weight in chair*)

...it depends.

CARLSON

In this case, petty officer Metcalf, who ordered you to prepare for and execute a covert mission to destroy the warehouses and pier in Sihanoukville [SEE-a-nook-vill] on June 6, 1970?

METCALF

(*Pauses, looks at Larkin*)

43

Do I have to answer that sir?

LARKIN

(*Nods yes*)

Yes.

METCALF

Lieutenant Kelly, my Naval Special Warfare Group DET [dett] Bravo executive officer. He said it had been determined in consultation with SOG, the Studies and Observations Group.

CARLSON

Did you have written orders to destroy the warehouses?

METCALF

(*Looks startled*)

Negative, sir. I've never received written orders for any of our missions during two tours in Vietnam.

CARLSON

Nor for missions in Cambodia, correct?

METCALF

Correct. Sir, these are TOP SECRET missions and we can't risk Team or DET [dett] security by having written mission orders floating around that could be compromised to the enemy by our

(*Makes quotation marks in the air with his fingers*)

"allies."

CARLSON

But the gist of your mission was to destroy the warehouses and pier because these new Cambodian allies could flip any day and start aiding communist forces again— correct?

METCALF

Basically.

CARLSON

Did you discuss at any time the effect that the loss of the port— the only deep water port in Cambodia— would have on the stability of the beleaguered Lon Nol [Lahn Nole] government— our ally?

METCALF

Loss of the port? We were only going to blow the warehouses—

CARLSON

With a nitrogen-enhanced weapon powerful enough to set off the explosives in the second warehouse!

METCALF

Yes...

CARLSON

You have EOD and nitrogen weapon training. Was there any doubt in your mind that the pier and quai [kway] wall would be destroyed in the process?

METCALF

Well, we looked at the location of the warehouses on charts and agent photos. It looked like they were far enough inland to spare the jetties and quai [kway] wall. Of course, once an ammo dump goes up, you can't tell what will happen...

CARLSON

Point out the warehouses on the chart, please.

METCALF

(*Points with crutch*)

CARLSON

Those are big warehouses, aren't they?

METCALF

Yes, sir— longer than a football field and a third as wide. You could fit two GARRISON COUNTYs in each of them.

CARLSON

And where was GARRISON COUNTY?

METCALF

(*Points with crutch*)

CARLSON

Seems pretty close, about half a ship length, correct?

                         METCALF

About.

                         CARLSON

But your original mission plan assumed GARRISON COUNTY would
be moored at the inner harbor, considerably further away
from the warehouses than where she moored at the quai wall,
correct?

                         METCALF
              (*Looks at harbor map, then quietly*)
Correct.

                         CARLSON

What about damage to GARRISON COUNTY?

                         METCALF

I thought we could get her out of there quickly before the
explosion.

                         CARLSON

You started the explosives timer around 1630, correct?

                         METCALF

Yes.

                         CARLSON

For a 30 minute delay time?

                         METCALF

Yes.

                         CARLSON

Did you ask the Commanding Officer of GARRISON COUNTY if he
could get his ship underway that fast?

                         METCALF

No, the mission was TOP SECRET. I just assumed he could...

                         CARLSON

So the possibility of destroying the pier at Sihanoukville
[SEE-a-nook-vill] and causing damage to GARRISON COUNTY was at
least generally discussed in preparation for your mission?

METCALF

Very generally. Our objective was to insure those communist weapons never got back into circulation to communist forces in Cambodia— no matter what the political situation.

CARLSON

Petty officer Metcalf, were you aware on June sixth that the Cambodian government had asked the United States to supply 2,000 M-2 carbine rifles to its marine battalions besieged by the North Vietnamese Army in the hills around Kep, Cambodia?

METCALF

(*Looks puzzled*)

No, sir.

CARLSON

Hypothetically, if this request for rifles existed and you knew about it, would it have changed your thinking about destroying the weapons in the warehouses at Sihanoukville [SEE-a-nook-vill]?

METCALF

I don't know— I can't answer that. That's a possibility I never discussed with anyone— if it's true.

(*Pauses*)

But I can tell you that we usually like to supply our formal allies with our own weapons, not the enemy's. That way if the allies decide to play footsie with the enemy units and sell the weapons to them, we know right away when it's our stuff they're shooting at us. If we supply them with enemy weaponry— AK-47s and the like— we never know where they came from, or if our allies are supplying them to the bad guys. So request for rifles or not, the warehouses still would better have been destroyed.

CARLSON

With whom did you discuss the possible consequences of your mission to destroy the warehouses at Sihanoukville [SEE-a-nook-vill]?

METCALF

Lieutenant Kelly.

CARLSON

Anyone else?

METCALF

No. He told me he had discussed it with his liaison at SOG, so everything was okay, and we should blow the warehouses regardless of collateral damage it might cause.

CARLSON

You said Phnom Penh [Nom-Pen] was under siege by North Vietnamese Army forces: The airport was closed, correct?

METCALF

Yes.

CARLSON

Even boat shipments of fuel, food and ammunition were suspended on the Mekong River for a time, correct?

METCALF

Yes.

CARLSON

With the port of Sihanoukville [SEE-a-nook-vill] out of order, Cambodia would be a dead duck from the standpoint of supply and logistics, correct?

METCALF

I... I don't know, sir. That's not my area of expertise.

CARLSON

Is it Lieutenant Kelly's area of expertise?

METCALF

I'm not sure sir. We just knew the mission had been OK'd by SOG.

CARLSON

Through Lieutenant Kelly, correct?

METCALF

Yes...

CARLSON

What is his full name and rank?

METCALF

Lieutenant

      (*shifts in his chair*)
junior grade

      (*everyone turns to look at Metcalf—*
      Kelly is only an Lieutenant Jaygee!)

William C. Kelly, USNR, SEAL Team One, DET [dett] Bravo
executive officer.

CARLSON

He's only a jaygee!

METCALF

Yes sir.

CARLSON

      (*Pauses to let the astonishing fact sink in with*
      Larkin, who keeps his eyes on Metcalf. Carlson
      walks back and forth behind counsel table for
      a few seconds, then turns to Metcalf)
One more thing: Did Lieutenant Medici [MEH-dih-chee] give you
a direct order to stop your mission to blow the warehouses?

METCALF

Sir, when an officer points a cocked nine millimeter pistol at
me and shouts "Cut the fucking wire!"— that's a direct order in
my book.

      (*Metcalf, Larkin, counsel and Medici*
      all laugh at this)

CARLSON

      (*Still smiling*)
Nothing further of this witness, your honor.

LARKIN

Very well, commander. Re-direct Colonel Breuner?

BREUNER

      (*Stands*)
Petty officer Metcalf, is there any doubt in your mind what

your covert mission orders were in Sihanoukville [SEE-a-nook-vill] on June 6th?

METCALF

No, sir— blow the warehouses on the pier if they contained communist weapons.

BREUNER

Did you accomplish that mission?

METCALF

No sir.

BREUNER

Why?

METCALF

Because Lieutenant Medici [MEH-dih-chee] interfered.

BREUNER

> (*Paces a few steps, stands behind Medici, then asks*
> *Metcalf*)

What's the prognosis on your leg, son?

METCALF

It's a deep wound and healing slowly. Fortunately Lieutenant Medici [MEH-dih-chee] missed the bone, but the doc says I'm out of field operations for good—

> (*Turns and glares at Medici*)

— SOG or SEAL.

BREUNER

No further questions.

LARKIN

Colonel Breuner, your next witness?

BREUNER

No further witnesses your honor. Judge Advocate rests.

LARKIN

Commander Carlson, your first witness.

CARLSON

Lieutenant Thomas N. Medici [MEH-dih-chee].

YEOMAN

(*Yoeman leads Medici to stand,
swears him with Bible*)
Do you solemnly swear that the testimony you are about to
give shall be the truth, the whole truth, and nothing but the
truth, so help you God?

MEDICI

I do.

(*Sits*)

CARLSON

Your full name?

MEDICI

Thomas N. Medici [MEH-dih-chee], Lieutenant, USNR, 7-2-8-4-7-1.

CARLSON

Your billet?

MEDICI

NILO Ha Tien [HAH-Tien]: Naval Intelligence Liaison Officer—
direct member of Admiral Zumwalt's Naval Forces Vietnam staff.
I report directly to Admiral Zumwalt and his Chief of Staff
for Intelligence.

CARLSON

Are you on independent naval duty?

MEDICI

Yes, sir. I have my own communications callsigns and
independent billet description.

CARLSON

What does that mean, Lieutenant?

MEDICI

It means I'm a completely independent duty station with a
complement of one— me— just like a ship is a completely
independent unit.

CARLSON

What's a NILO?

MEDICI

NILOs perform independent field intelligence collection and analysis, both with their own eyes and ears, and through reports of their field agents. We also coordinate intelligence efforts— "liaise" [lee-ayes]— with our Vietnamese and American military and civilian counterparts in the intelligence community.

CARLSON

Such as...?

MEDICI

I attend a daily DIOCC [Die-Ock] meeting in Ha Tien [HAH-Tien] with the Vietnamese District Chief, the local Regional Force commander, the local Chief of National Police, the local Vietnamese Navy NILO.

CARLSON

Do you do any original intelligence collection work?

MEDICI

Yes, sir. I manage a naval spy network of agents called Collection Team 5— CT-5. I receive and process their reports through a principal-interpreter— the net handler. This network has been expanded during my time in Ha Tien [HAH-Tien] to cover the Vietnam-Cambodia border from the Gulf of Thailand to the Bassac [Bah-sock] River, and north along the Cambodian coast all the way to Thailand.

CARLSON

Where is Ha Tien [HAH-Tien]? Can you point it out on the map?

MEDICI

(*Points to Ha Tien on large map of
Indo-China*)

Smack dab on the Vietnam-Cambodian border where it hits the Gulf of Thailand. We are WAAAY out there. Kind of the Barstow of Vietnam.

CARLSON

Do you have any direct access to any other original

intelligence reports?

MEDICI

Yes. I board with Frank Brown, an army warrant officer who runs the 5-2-5 Military Intelligence Group outpost in Ha Tien [HAH-Tien]. He and I are very good friends and colleagues. We share a lot of original intel product and work on new collection schemes and tasking for our agents. We also devise collection missions where I do the collection personally— where ever I need to go...

CARLSON

I thought your area of operations was the Ha Tien [HAH-Tien] area in Vietnam?

MEDICI

It was— is. I try daily to brief whatever American patrol boats are in the area about any specific threats that our agents uncover, before the boats go on night ambush.

CARLSON

Where do they patrol?

MEDICI

The Vinh Te [Vinn Tay] Canal along the Vietnam-Cambodia border, and the Rach Giang Thanh [Rock Yang Tahn] River connecting it to the Gulf. We are in the area the North Vietnamese Army calls its Military Region 3— where all the weapons and ammunition for the Mekong Delta come into Vietnam from Cambodia. The patrol boats' job is to intercept those weapons shipments.

CARLSON

Has your job changed at all since you've been NILO Ha Tien [HAH-Tien]— since the beginning of 1970?

MEDICI

Yes, a lot. My collection efforts have gone from local to more broadly strategic— where the stuff is landed, stored, shipped and infiltrated through Cambodia into Vietnam.

CARLSON

Precisely to stop this infiltration is why we conducted an invasion— excuse me— "incursion" into Cambodia in April of this year, correct?

MEDICI

Yes, sir. We tried to mop up the communist supply depots along the Cambodian side of the border— the "sanctuaries." You'll recall that former head of state Prince Sihanouk [SEE-a-nook] professed Cambodian neutrality, while looking the other way from North Vietnamese Army supply activities on the border with Vietnam.

CARLSON

What do you mean your job changed to focus more on "strategic" intelligence?

MEDICI

Political intelligence. For instance, Frank Brown recruited as an agent the Recording Secretary of the new Cambodian Cabinet—

(*Larkin, Breuner, mouths open, stare in disbelief*)

LARKIN

I order everyone here to treat this information as TOP SECRET special intelligence, and not repeat it to anyone outside this room. The agent's life may depend on it.

MEDICI

Not necessary, Captain. He was killed at the end of May. I saw him get it.

LARKIN

I still don't want the information repeated outside this room. Continue, Lieutenant.

MEDICI

We were the first to hear and report that Prince Sihanouk [SEE-a-nook] was ousted as head of state by his cousin, the parliamentary leader, Sirik Matak [Seer-EEK Mah-TOCK], and replaced by the government of the Lon brothers— Lon Nol [Lahn Nole] and Lon Non.

CARLSON

Why is political intelligence so important from Cambodia?

MEDICI

Because the new Lon Nol [Lahn Nole] government has stopped communist weapons shipments into Sihanoukville [SEE-a-nook-vill] from Singapore and elsewhere on Soviet and Chinese ships. Certain Cambodian generals— including Lon Nol [Lahn Nole] and Lon Non— used to receive half the weapons which were imported into Sihanoukville [SEE-a-nook-vill] to sell to whomever they wanted. That was the bribe necessary so the other half could be shipped down to the border into Vietnam for the Vietcong and North Vietnamese Army units there.

(*Medici sits straight up.*)

The point is, that traffic has stopped completely in the last three months due to the goodwill of the new, shaky Cambodian regime— and possibly some payments from the CIA. To their credit the Lon brothers have resisted all inducements by the communists to resume shipments— resisted the offer to accept the former half-share bribe; resisted the offer by the Chinese to insure that the popular deposed leader, Prince Sihanouk [SEE-a-nook], "has a plane crash"— their words, not mine— while in China under asylum, in order to eliminate popular resistance to the new Lon regime. And they are now resisting— barely— North Vietnamese efforts to capture Phnom Penh [Nom-Pen] by closing the airport, blockading the Mekong, destroying Radio Phnom Penh [Nom-Pen], and cutting off petroleum imports to the country.

MEDICI
(*Turns to Larkin*)
This is one shaky but steadfast government. Its survival means the North Vietnamese and Viet Cong units in the delta will die a slow death of attrition from the weapons cutoff. That's why insuring the survival of Cambodia— and this government— is so important.

CARLSON
How do you know all this?

MEDICI
From my agents, from 5-2-5 Military Intelligence agents, and discussions with intel staff in Saigon.

CARLSON
Any input from civilian agencies?

MEDICI

I speak periodically with the CIA regional chief— one way: he asks, I report. Never much from them. We heard that they have no agents in Cambodia, so have to debrief refugees coming across the border at Ha Tien [HAH-Tien], and steal what they can from us.

CARLSON

Why do you speak with them if they offer nothing?

MEDICI

Because I was ordered to by the US Ambassador! Our Cambodian intelligence was so good— or the CIA had so little— that I was ordered to limit distribution of my reports only to the CIA station chief, to General Abrams, Admiral Zumwalt, and the White House Situation Room. I had to cut out my zone boss, and it pissed him off and got me in hot water.

CARLSON

Are you consulted by anyone on Cambodian matters?

MEDICI

All the time. I'm jokingly called "Our man in Cambodia." Civilian, Army and Navy intelligence brass come up to Ha Tien [HAH-Tien] regularly for briefings or for me to be their tour guide in border Cambodia. That's how I met John Paul Vann [van]...

BREUNER

I object, your honor. This discussion is irrelevant to what Lieutenant Medici [MEH-dih-chee] did on June 6.

CARLSON

Not at all your honor. I'm painting the picture of what the senior officer present in the warehouses— Lieutenant Medici [MEH-dih-chee]— knew at the time of the incident which compelled him to act as he did.

LARKIN

I agree with Colonel Breuner that this testimony seems to be getting far afield, but upon Commander Carlson's offer of its relevance, I'm inclined to let the witness continue— but not until we take a break.

(*Looks around*)

56

It's too damn hot in here. I'll see how the techs are doing with the air conditioner. Recess for ten minutes, gentlemen.

(*Raps his gavel; Larkin leaves; Breuner, Carlson, Medici and Metcalf in room*)

O'NEILL
(*Walks up to Medici*)
Don't think you're going to get away with this, Lieutenant. You goddam reserves come into the Navy with your outrageous conduct and ideas...

CARLSON
(*Steps in front of O'Neill, face to face.*)
That's enough, Commander. I ask you as gentleman to restrain your remarks and leave him alone. Your lawyer will have his chance at him on cross-examination.

O'NEILL
(*O'Neill gives one last contemptuous look at Medici, then faces Carlson, starts to say something, then walks away briskly, and mutters.*)
Slick bastard!

MEDICI
(*Hangdog look, head down, when Breuner is gone.*)
Is Breuner going to rip me on cross-examination?

CARLSON
I don't know. He's seen all your service reports and claims to have talked to the people you worked with. He's very thorough. I hope you've been candid with me about any other boo-boos you made up there...

MEDICI
(*Sits up, nervous*)
Do you think he's talked to Redkin— about the mortar ammunition...

CARLSON
I don't know. I've been unable to contact Redkin. They said he was out on patrol.

MEDICI
Is Larkin getting the point?

57

CARLSON

(*Looks blankly at the empty dais.*)

I hope so.

(*Goes out steel door.*)

YEOMAN

(*Approaches Medici*)

Excuse me, Mr. Medici [MEH-dih-chee]. The intel boss asked me to make sure you still want to be considered for deep selection by the Lieutenant Commander Promotion Board. It meets in Washington next week, and we'll need to assemble all your fitness reports and certificates for all your medals if you still want to be considered.

MEDICI

Yes, I still want to be considered by the Lieutenant Commander Board. Please have them put the package together.

YEOMAN

But the boss thought, with the Inquiry and all, you might want to wait...

MEDICI

(*Explodes*)

Godammit, yeoman! What part of "yes" don't you understand?

YEOMAN

(*Backing away*)

Aye-aye, sir.

MEDICI

(*Turns, finds himself looking at Metcalf who sits in a chair with crutches on table. He and Metcalf try to avoid each other's stare, then look directly at each other, Medici vacant, Metcalf with anger.*)

METCALF

(*Metcalf tries to stand, falters on his wounded leg and falls back into chair, defeated by pain. Then he raises one crutch and smashes it on the counsel table with a resounding crack.*)

You bastard!

MEDICI
(*Hangs head down.*)

(*Lights down.*)

INTERMISSION

ACT TWO

SCENE 1

(Lights up. Scene: Same. Medici on stand. Carlson continues questioning. Larkin, Breuner, Metcalf, and Yeoman seated at tables)

CARLSON

Lieutenant, do you speak any languages?

MEDICI

English, French, Vietnamese, southern dialect.

CARLSON

In what language are your field agent reports from your network?

MEDICI

French— written on rice paper by the principal interpreter— the man who recruits the agents, pays them and solicits weekly information, then delivers the reports to me. I also receive reports from the Vietnamese NILO of Vietnamese and Khmer agents— those are translated into French.

CARLSON

How can you understand these reports?

MEDICI

Commander, I'm fluent in French, that's why I was sent to Ha Tien [HAH-Tien]. I'm an honors graduate of Princeton in Politics, with a minor in French. Almost all the Cambodes were either educated in French at local lycees [lee-say], or in France, or used French in dealings with the old colonial government. I'm quite good at the language.

CARLSON

How do you judge that?

MEDICI

Well, I'm good enough that I was able to negotiate the weapons deal with the Cambodian Navy for their Marine battalions at

60

Kep. I got a medal for it!

CARLSON

Tell us about that.

MEDICI

A Cambodian Navy corvette sailed into Vietnamese waters off Ha Tien [HAH-Tien] in April and signalled our LST to send an interpreter. Captain Brown of USS WHITFIELD COUNTY called me on the radio and asked me to come talk to them. I rode out on a patrol boat to the Cambodian ship. I was received cordially by Captain Som Sary, and I instructed the boat to leave, that I would be okay.

CARLSON

This was before we knew the Cambodians had decided to switch sides, correct?

MEDICI

Yes— but I had been in Cambodia before and I trusted the people. I trusted Som Sary. We spoke, finally, in French for four hours, and he made the official request from Lon Nol [Lahn Nole] for 2,000 M-2 carbines from the U.S. to save their Marine battalions surrounded by North Vietnamese units at Kep, Cambodia, about 20 kilometers north of the Vietnam border. They were desperate. We knew the North Vietnamese had begun to physically take control of the border areas of Cambodia to continue their weapons shipments regardless of whose side the new government took.

CARLSON

What did you do?

MEDICI

I returned to Captain Brown's ship, sent a TOP SECRET FLASH message to Saigon with the request, and waited— and waited. Finally Som Sary had to get underway back to the Cambodian naval base at Ream [Ray-emm] near Sihanoukville [SEE-a-nook-vill], and said he would return in two days. I heard nothing back from Saigon for two days, then just a short message from intel staff saying "Everything A-OK," nothing else. Som Sary came back, I went aboard and reported Saigon's response. Som Sary just smiled and said "Okay, je le comprends. C'est okay." He then took me on a tour of the Cambodian coast on his ship for a few days. I did some reconn and found their maps and charts— old French jobs— to be inaccurate. We returned to An Thoi [ANN-toy], I got off and Som Sary steamed back to Cambodia. And I didn't see him again— until Sihanoukville [SEE-a-nook-vill].

(*Larkin turns and looks at Medici, puzzled.*)

CARLSON

What about the 2,000 rifles?

MEDICI

I didn't know what happened, since no one reported back to me. But when I flew to Phu Quoc [Foo-Kwock] Island to catch the GARRISON COUNTY for the Sihanoukville [SEE-a-nook-vill] mission, there was a big black Air Force CONEX container by the airstrip. I asked the NILO there what that was, and he said "I'm not sure. Probably an installment of the rifles the CIA has been delivering to Cambodia by Air America planes."

BREUNER

Objection, hearsay.

CARLSON

Your honor, offered for LIEUTENANT Medici [MEH-dih-chee]'s state of mind when he did what followed. May I continue?

LARKIN

Yes, let's see where you're going with this.

CARLSON

What did you do next, Lieutenant?

MEDICI

I examined the CONEX container, which was heavily sealed. Stencilled in new paint on its side was "Carbines, M-2, 500 each." I concluded that the CIA had made good on the delivery of the weapons.

(*Larkin, Breuner, Metcalf now all listening, rapt.*)

CARLSON

(*Pauses, walks back and forth
behind counsel table, then stops*)
OK, Lieutenant. And you did all the negotiations with the

62

Cambodians in French language, as well as your agent reports being in French?

MEDICI

Yes.

CARLSON

Now, what precisely was YOUR mission to Sihanoukville [SEE-a-nook-vill] on June 6th, 1970?

MEDICI

To conduct a port survey using personnel of GARRISON COUNTY, and to ascertain HOW to take out the port of Sihanoukville [SEE-a-nook-vill] IF we had to.

LARKIN
(Looks puzzled.)
Not to destroy the port, Lieutenant?

MEDICI
(Turns to Larkin.)
No sir, not then. I was trying to say before, these negotiations were going on with the Cambodes. The new government had stopped the enemy weapons shipments into Sihanoukville [SEE-a-nook-vill] and we were doing all we could to shore up the government against the all-out attack by the North Vietnamese— which began as soon as they knew the weapons shipments had stopped. The Mekong was blockaded on and off for supplies to Phnom Penh [Nom-Pen]— Ponchetong airport was closed to air traffic— all they had left was the Port of Sihanoukville [SEE-a-nook-vill]. We knew Cambodia might fall, and then we might have to destroy the port. But until that happened we HAD to keep the port open as a last means of supply. We had plans laid to run convoys up Route 2 to Phnom Penh [Nom-Pen]. It would be difficult and dangerous, but a last resort to save the new government. That's why I was sent to obtain information on the port.

And that's the intellectual reason I knew something was out of whack when I saw what Metcalf was attempting to do.

CARLSON
You said "intellectual reason." Was there another reason?

MEDICI
(*Turns back to Carlson.*)
Yes— intuitive. Commander Holland, my boss in Saigon, would have told me about the SOG plan to blow the warehouses. I believed to a certainty he would never have led me into a mission with that kind of risk without informing me, regardless of its security classification. What's more, he never would send me on a merely academic mission. If he knew the port was to be blown, why send me to find out how to do it?

CARLSON
Any other reason?

MEDICI
USS GARRISON COUNTY. They wouldn't risk that ship and those men so close to the explosion of a major ammo dump without making sure the ship was well clear in plenty of time. That's how we do things on intelligence staff.
(*Larkin makes a note.*)

CARLSON
(*Carlson walks around behind the counsel table*
to let the last answer sink in, then continues)
Lieutenant, did you accomplish your mission to Sihanoukville [SEE-a-nook-vill]?

MEDICI
Yes, but barely.

CARLSON
What do you mean?

MEDICI
We accomplished the port survey part fine on the way in, photographed the piers, warehouses, quai [kway] wall, sounded the channel, precisely plotted the location of all navigational marks.
(*Clears his throat, shifts in his chair.*)

This is where it really starts to sound goofy. I went ashore shortly after the dignitaries were received on GARRISON COUNTY when we berthed that morning. I waited for a taxi at the foot of the piers in my civilian clothes, with a camera, but without a weapon. I was trying to be a tourist best I could, for a

64

Caucasian wandering around Sihanoukville [SEE-a-nook-vill].
Then who of all people drives by, but Captain Som Sary of the
Cambodian naval ship— the guy I had negotiated the weapons
deal with. He's in a navy jeep with his Exec. I'm devastated—
my mission is blown— they know who I am and likely why I'm
there. In a flash I get paranoid, calculating how they knew I
would be there, were they setting me up, like that.

They see me and are all smiles, shouts and waves. They stop
and ask me if I need a ride, where am I going? I say just
around town, a little *"tourisme,"* some *"photographie"*. They say
"Bon! We will take you— a friend of Cambodia."

I try to beg off but they graciously insist I come with them.
I get in. They drive me all around the port and city, take me
to eat, to see the hotel and casino, take photos at all the
tourist spots. More food, more drink. I think my mission is
sunk. We buy batik material so I can have some cool Cambodian
bermuda shorts. I buy them gas at the ESSO station. We have a
jolly good time, and I've concluded they probably don't want to
kill me, because of the weapons deal.

> (*Clears his throat, shifts his
> weight in chair*)

We end the afternoon at a cafe overlooking the new walled
harbor— the one built by the French to protect berthed ships
from the dangerous swell of the southwest monsoon. There's
an odd craft anchored in the harbor that we watch. The port
captain of Sihanoukville [SEE-a-nook-vill] joins us at our
table. Som Sary tells him what a friend of Cambodia I am. I
ask what the funny little ship is. He says a French suction
dredge that breaks down constantly. A gift to Cambodia to
protect the harbor from currents that silt it up so fast it
must be dredged each week or the harbor would be rendered
useless in only six weeks! French engineering! Aiyee!

> (*Medici sits up, looks at the Board and smiles.*)

BINGO! There it was, at the end of my tourist day, the elegant
answer of how to take out the port: sink the dredge and the
harbor will silt up and become useless.

(Larkin smiles, but shakes his head.)

CARLSON
So your mission was accomplished. What did you do then?

MEDICI
They drop me off at GARRISON COUNTY. I find Metcalf gone and in the warehouses. I get my Browning— I just know something's not right— run down to the warehouses and I find him there ready to explode them. All this goes through my mind about saving the new Cambodian government and about Commander Holland not putting me in this predicament.

(Looks directly at Metcalf)

I yelled at Metcalf to cut the wire— then the shouting in the warehouse, Metcalf threw something, hit my head, and was on top of me— and the pistol went off.

(Deflates, looks at Larkin with a far-away, spent look, then speaks quietly, with humility)

It seems incredible to me as I relate it here today.

CARLSON
Do you know what, if anything, happened to the weapons in those warehouses SINCE June sixth?

MEDICI
Yes. My agent reported—

(Looks at Metcalf)

in French—

(Turns back to Larkin)

that they were all trucked out over twelve nights to Governor Um Samuth's [OOM-Samoot's] palace in Bokor [Boe-core] Province in the Elephant Mountains southeast of Sihanoukville [SEE-a-nook-vill], where they are under constant guard by the

Cambodian Army. He counted the trucks and saw the cases being removed from the warehouses— and one night rode with the trucks to Bokor [Boe-core].

> (*Medici reaches into his pocket and pulls out a rice paper report with French writing on it.*)

I have the report right here—

BREUNER

Objection— hearsay.

CARLSON

Business records exception— Lieutenant Medici's [MED-ih-chee's] agent reports are business records maintained in the normal course of business— intelligence collection for Naval staff.

LARKIN

Overruled.

CARLSON

Forces of the government friendly to U.S. efforts, Lieutenant?

MEDICI

Yes. The Cambodes moved them inland to Bokor where they would be less exposed to— let me translate—

> (*Reads soto voce in French from rice paper report*)

"...*opérations de cowboy pour les détruire par les unites secrètes du gouvernement des États-Unis*"—

> (*Looks at Carlson, in full voice*)

"Where they would be less exposed to cowboy operations to destroy them by secret units of the U.S. government."— Their words, not mine.

LARKIN

> (*Shakes his head in exasperation*)

Goddam French never left this place.

CARLSON

Your honor, could we take a short break?

LARKIN

Yes. Do you have more questions for Lieutenant Medici [MEH-dih-chee]?

CARLSON

I think I can finish quickly with him after the break, your honor.

LARKIN

Colonel Breuner, are you ready to cross-examine Lieutenant Medici [MEH-dih-chee] when we resume?

BREUNER

Yes, your honor— READY!

LARKIN

(*Taps gavel*)
We'll take a fifteen minute recess.

(*Larkin, Breuner and Metcalf leave room.*)

MEDICI

Breuner didn't put on any evidence of the violation of the Presidential Order about no ammunition to the Cambodes— does that mean he dropped it?

CARLSON

Maybe, but he's smart. I think he's saving it for your cross-examination. To help him with his other charges.

MEDICI

(*Medici stands up from witness chair, stretches and smiles at Carlson. Steps down.*)

CARLSON

What are you smiling at Lieutenant? You look like the Cheshire cat.

MEDICI

We got my story out, didn't we?

CARLSON

Yes, but I'm not sure Larkin looks at it the same way you do. All this agent report bullshit, your trips into Cambodia with

these naval officers— illegal and in violation of neutrality—
and who knows what the Cambodes motives are? You live in a
different world than line officers.

                    MEDICI

          (*Incensed, full of hubris.*)
I AM a line officer, Commander. I'm doing this job because I
asked for it, and it needs to be done with some finesse, not
just blowing shit up all the time. I was a director officer
on USS TULSA. I blew stuff up all the time with her six inch
guns. You may think this is a fruitcake job. But it's real, and
it makes a difference.

                    CARLSON
          (*Turning to leave room.*)
Let's hope Larkin thinks so.

               (*Carlson leaves room. Yeoman
                approaches Medici, hesitant*)

                    YEOMAN
Lieutenant, Intel boss sent this note about the Lieutenant-
commander Promotion Board...

                    MEDICI
Dammit, man! YES!— I want my files in front of that Board next
week! I could become the youngest Lieutenant-commander in the
Navy's history...

                    YEOMAN
Sir, you just need to sign this file release form. That's all I
meant.

                    MEDICI

          (*Glares at Yeoman, grabs papers,
          scribbles signature, slaps pen on
          the papers, and walks off.*)

          (*Lights down.*)

ACT TWO

SCENE 2

(*Lights up. Larkin, Carlson, Metcalf
seated, Medici on witness stand
being cross-examined by Breuner,
standing.*)

BREUNER

Lieutenant, what's an order to you?

MEDICI

Sir?

BREUNER

What is a military order to you? Define it.

MEDICI

When a superior officer in my chain of command directs me to
do or not do something, I obey.

BREUNER

Well, what about your standing orders from N-2, the staff, and
Admiral Zumwalt. Do you obey them?

MEDICI

Yes sir.

BREUNER

When they tell you not to go into Cambodia by yourself—

MEDICI

(*Squirms in chair.*)
They never really ORDER me NOT to go...

BREUNER

Have you ever discussed directly with Commander Holland, or
the Chief of Staff for Intel, or Admiral Zumwalt your forays
into Cambodia, and their views about your actions?

MEDICI

(*Looks at Carlson*)
Not directly.

BREUNER

Indirectly?

MEDICI
(*Looks at Carlson for guidance;
Carlson just sits there calmly.*)
I guess so.

BREUNER

You GUESS so?

(*Picks up a folder of message reports*)

You have sent reports of your forays into Cambodia—
before the Sihanoukville [SEE-a-nook-vill] mission— to
Naval Intel staff and others, correct?

MEDICI

Yes.

BREUNER
Cambodia was a neutral country in this war when you went
to Ha Tien [HAH-Tien] in January 1970, correct?

MEDICI
Well, technically...

BREUNER
What do our Rules of Engagement say about entering
Cambodian territory or shooting into Cambodia?

MEDICI
That we are not permitted on Cambodian territory unless
we are first shot at from Cambodia, then we may enter
Cambodia and shoot back in hot pursuit.

BREUNER
The "Hot Pursuit" exception, right?

MEDICI
Yes. But we all know Cambodia was not really neutral,
because Prince Sihanouk [SEE-a-nook] turned a blind eye
to the North Vietnamese shipping weapons into Vietnam
across the border, and in fact we knew communist weapons

were being brought into Sihanoukville [SEE-a-nook-vill] by the shipload for transport into Vietnam.

BREUNER
Something of a dilemma, right?

MEDICI
Of course. But we need to know what's going on in Cambodia— so I go in.

BREUNER
So that dilemma is your justification for illegal entries into Cambodia in violation of the Rules of Engagement?

CARLSON
Objection. Question states a legal conclusion, that any particular entry into Cambodia violated the Rules of Engagement.

LARKIN
Sustained— Colonel, please limit your questions to specifics.

CARLSON
It's also irrelevant to what happened on June sixth.

BREUNER
But not to this officer's state of mind about what his ACTUAL orders are, and WHETHER he obeys them.

LARKIN
(*Looks peevishly at Medici.*)
You may continue this line of questioning about specifics, if you have them, Colonel.

BREUNER
Lieutenant Medici [MEH-dih-chee], you admit that you have entered Cambodia numerous times since January 1970, correct?

MEDICI
(*Very quietly*)
Yes.

BREUNER
Did anyone on naval staff ever discuss with you your expeditions into Cambodia?

MEDICI

They might have...

BREUNER

Did Captain Ross, your Chief of Staff for Intelligence, ever discuss these expeditions with you?

MEDICI

Yes.

BREUNER

Didn't he tell you they were illegal, and that if you were caught there, the Navy would have to disavow you and your mission?

MEDICI

What I remember is that he said my expeditions were "cheeky." He says stuff like that.

BREUNER

Did he warn you of consequences of getting caught?

MEDICI

I think so— but he also said he was pleased at the original intel I was getting from those trips.

BREUNER

How about Commander Holland— your mentor at N-2. Didn't he warn you what you were doing was illegal?

MEDICI
(*Flushed at mention of Commander Holland*)
I didn't take it as a lecture on the legality of what I do. I took it as his sincere personal concern for my safety, and staff's inability to help me if I got caught.

BREUNER

So you never saw those warnings as ORDERS not to go into Cambodia?

MEDICI

No. They were NOT orders. They were cautions.

BREUNER

Let me ask you some specifics, Lieutenant—

(Opens file, picks up one sheet and reads.)
Did you on February 18, 1970 debark River Patrol Boat 14 of
River Division 532, with Lieutenant jaygee Marks as officer in
charge, on the Cambodian side of the Giang Thanh [Yang Tahn]
River at the border, and walk armed into the Cambodian hamlet
of Ton Hon?

MEDICI

I don't remember the exact date. But yes, I did.

BREUNER

Did you have orders to go into Ton Hon?

MEDICI

I was tasked to see how much diesel fuel was for sale there in
the market— we suspected that over fifty percent of the diesel
we supplied to the South Vietnamese is sold on the black
market at the border and ends up in North Vietnamese hands. So
I guess in a way I was ordered to find out about the diesel,
and the only way to do it first hand was to go in. Since we
were there, we laid sensors on the way out along the trails
the Red Star Transportation Battalion used to cross the river
at night.

BREUNER

But no direct orders from N-2 or anyone else, correct?

MEDICI

Correct.

BREUNER

*(Takes another sheet of paper from the file and
reads.)*
Did you in early March 1970 call in Naval gunfire from the U.S.
Coast Guard cutter Kodiak onto Nui Dai Dung [Nooey Die Young]
mountain on the Cambodian border?

MEDICI

(Squirms)
Yes, but there had been enemy trucks transporting weapons in
and around the mountain, and we never could reach them with
the four deuce mortar at Ha Tien [HAH-Tien]. The cutter was
shallow draft and could get in close enough to shoot them up.

BREUNER

Did not some of the rounds go long over Dai Dung [Die Young]
into Cambodia?

MEDICI

Probably.

BREUNER

Were you under orders to shoot into Cambodia?

MEDICI

No.

BREUNER

Was the action in hot pursuit?

MEDICI

No.

BREUNER
(*Takes another sheet from folder*)
Lieutenant, Do you know Warrant Officer third Stan Zablocki?

MEDICI

Yes.

BREUNER

Did you not organize with him a "Navy Fire Team" to man an
81MM mortar at points around the Ha Tien [HAH-Tien] peninsula?

MEDICI

Yes, we did. To have some land based naval firepower so we
wouldn't have to rely on the Army in emergencies.

BREUNER

Was there such an emergency on March 12, 1970, when you and
your fire team set up near Thach Dong [Tack Dong] Regional
Force outpost and placed mortar fire on the slopes of Nui Dai
Dung [Nooey Die Young] mountain?

MEDICI

Well, it was— kind of. The North Vietnamese Army had been
moving weapons around the back of the mountain, which would
all end up in Vietnam and used against us. We tried to shake

them up at night.

                           BREUNER
On the Vietnam or Cambodian side of the mountain?

                           MEDICI
Well, probably both.

                           BREUNER
In hot pursuit?

                           MEDICI
Not exactly.

                           BREUNER
What happened to you on the thirteenth of March?

                           MEDICI
I don't remember.

                           BREUNER
You don't remember the combat action for which you were
awarded a Bronze Star?

                           MEDICI
            (*Sheepish*)
Oh, that day. We drove up to the border to see what damage
our fire team had done with the mortar the day before. We had
seen secondary explosions and wanted to see what we hit. Frank
Brown drove out with me during the afternoon. Before we got to
the border—

            (*Sits up, excited*)

the North Vietnamese on Dai Dung [Die Young] started mortaring
us! We spent the afternoon and evening in a ditch. The major
declared it a "Tac-E"— tactical emergency— and we had all
kinds of aircraft up from Canh Tho [Can-Toe] bombing the
bejeesus out of Nui Dai Dung [Nooey Die Young]. I acted
as forward air controller till the real ones got there to
continue the bombing.

                           BREUNER
All in hot pursuit, correct?

MEDICI

Yeah, I guess that was actual hot pursuit of fire from Cambodia.

BREUNER

And how long did it continue?

MEDICI

Umm— about two weeks, day and night. There was little left of the North Vietnamese caves on either side of Die Young when the bombing ended.

BREUNER

And all based on your unsolicited fire into Cambodia, in violation of the Rules of Engagement on March 12, correct?

MEDICI

I guess you could look at it that way.

BREUNER

Were you proud of that, Lieutenant?

MEDICI

Proud? No.

But the weapons infiltration stopped at Ha Tien [HAH-Tien], and we sure slept a lot better at night from then on!
> (*Larkin and Carlson stifle snickers, Breuner looks
> peeved*)

BREUNER

> (*Takes another sheet of paper and reads.*)

BREUNER

Do you know a Gunnersmate Second Class Redkin?

MEDICI

> (*Looks at Carlson, shrinks into witness chair.*)

Yes, he runs the armory for the river division at Ha Tien [HAH-Tien].

BREUNER

He is responsible for all the navy weapons and ammunition stored in Ha Tien [HAH-Tien], correct?

MEDICI

Yes.

BREUNER

Do you remember obtaining from Redkin six cases of 60 mike-mike mortar ammunition— two high explosive, two white phosphorous, and two air burst— on March 28, 1970?

MEDICI

I'm not sure of the date or amounts...

BREUNER

(*Holds up blue canvas-covered navy logbook.*)
Would it refresh your recollection to see Redkin's detailed armorer's log regarding the date and details?

MEDICI

No. I assume Redkin's entry is correct.

BREUNER

What did you tell Redkin the mortar shells were for?

MEDICI

A special operation we were doing next day.

BREUNER

In fact didn't you provide that ammunition to the Cambodian District Chief of Kampong Trach [Campong Track] district along the border?

MEDICI

That was the purpose of getting the shells— but I don't know for sure that they got to him...

BREUNER

(*Takes another sheet from file*)
Do you remember an Air America helo pilot named Ned Anderson?

MEDICI

Uhhh— was he the guy who flew the stuff into Kampong Trach?

BREUNER

That's the guy...

MEDICI

Yes, I loaded the six cases into an Air America helo for direct delivery— I was told— to the Kampong Trach District Chief.

BREUNER

Did not Anderson remind you that giving ammo to the Cambodes violated a Presidential Order?

MEDICI
(*Nervously*)

Ahh, maybe...

BREUNER

To which you responded with the "Fuck Nixon and his Kraut" remark?

MEDICI
(*Meekly*)

Yes.

BREUNER

And this happened on or about March 29, 1970?

MEDICI
(*Dejected*)

Yes, the day after I got the ammo from Redkin.

BREUNER
(*Takes out a naval message*)

Lieutenant Medici [MEH-dih-chee], do you remember receiving this ALL COMMANDS message to your communications address on or about March 20, 1970, nine days before this ammo transfer?
(*Flips a copy to Carlson, hands one to Larkin, shows original to Medici*)

MEDICI
(*Dejected, reads message cursorily, but knows what it is*)

I think so...

BREUNER

Please read it out loud.

MEDICI

(*Mumbles*)

From Commander in Chief, blah-blah-blah...

BREUNER

Out loud, Lieutenant!

MEDICI

It's from "CINC— Commander in Chief— the President— to ALL COMMANDS, Vietnam" Dated March 20, 1970, and it requires us to "NOT, repeat NOT, provide ammunition or weapons to Cambodian forces during this critical period of review of Cambodian-U.S. relations."

BREUNER

Were you aware of this message before you caused the mortar shells to be provided to the Kampong Trach [Campong Track] District Chief?

CARLSON

Objection— I must assert the Lieutenant's Fifth Amendment privilege against self-incrimination...

LARKIN

I believe he has waived the privilege, commander, by taking the stand.

CARLSON

Then I also object because the line of questioning is irrelevant— Colonel Breuner put on no evidence of the violation of the Presidential Order in his case in chief. I therefore move to dismiss that charge.

LARKIN

That motion was appropriate at the close of Colonel Breuner's case.

CARLSON

I could have made the motion your honor, but I assumed Colonel Breuner had abandoned the charge. I would have advised Lieutenant Medici [MEH-dih-chee] differently if I had known Colonel Breuner had intended to question Lieutenant Medici [MEH-dih-chee] about it. So my position is that you should either grant the dismissal of that charge, and rule Colonel Breuner's questions on it irrelevant, or you permit the question, and allow me to advise my client of his Fifth Amendment rights on this specific issue.

LARKIN

Well, I'm inclined to allow the question, and the Privilege is personal— Do you wish to assert it Lieutenant Medici [MEH-dih-chee]?

MEDICI

(*Looks at Carlson, looks down*)

No your honor, I do not assert it.

CARLSON

Your honor, may I have a moment to counsel my client?

MEDICI

Commander, I'm okay.

(*Turns to Larkin, looks unburdened*)

Sir, the North Vietnamese were overrunning Kampong Trach [Campong Track] District in the days immediately after Prince Sihanouk [SEE-a-nook] was deposed, in order to physically gain control of the border areas of Cambodia to continue their weapons movement into Vietnam. The district chief was an ally of ours for years. He reported regularly on North Vietnamese Army weapons movements at the border in his district, at great personal risk. He had virtually no local troops or weapons, or ammunition— a few rifles and a 60 millimeter mortar. We thought the least we could do was send him some ammo to defend himself until Dr. Kissinger decided what to do about Cambodia after his "critical period of review." Don't forget, we didn't invade the border sanctuaries in Cambodia till April 30th, almost six weeks after Sihanouk [SEE-a-nook] was deposed— a long six weeks.

(*Turns to Breuner*)

I heard the mortar shells helped him hold off the North Vietnamese units till then...

CARLSON

(*On his feet, upset by Medici's [MED-ih-chee's] confessional rambling*)

Your honor, may we take a break?

LARKIN

Yes, ten minutes.
>
> (*Larkin, Breuner, Metcalf leave. Carlson stares at Medici*)

MEDICI
>
> (*Rocking back and forth in chair catatonically, singing to himself, to the tune of "Shortenin' Bread"*)

MEDICI

Momma's little NILO gonna Portsmouth, Portsmouth,
Momma's little NILO gonna Portsmouth shed.
Momma's little NILO gonna Portsmouth, Portsmouth,
Momma's little NILO gonna end up dead!

CARLSON

What the hell are you doing? Breuner put on no evidence of this charge, and you spill it all out! We discussed this possibility, and I told you to hold up what you were saying if you heard me raise the Fifth Amendment Privilege so I would have a chance to counsel you.

MEDICI

The hell with it. I did it, I knew it was wrong, and I even joked about it. And I would do it again to save one of our guys. That's my war, commander, whether you and the Board like it or not!

CARLSON
>
> (*Shakes his head, walks slowly to the door, turns*)

You are one stubborn bastard, Lieutenant!

MEDICI
>
> (*Laughs*)

Now everyone agrees on at least one thing— I'm a bastard!

> (*Lights fade.*)

ACT TWO

SCENE 3

(*Lights up. Scene: Same: Larkin, Carlson, Metcalf seated, Medici on witness stand, Breuner standing*)

CARLSON
(*Stands, speaks to Larkin*)

Your honor, for the record, I'm going to renew my motion that the Judge Advocate's request for a specification on the charge that Lieutenant Medici [MEH-dih-chee] violated a direct Presidential Order be stricken. Colonel Breuner put on no evidence of it in his case in chief, and I could have asked for a dismissal when Colonel Breuner rested his case. But in the interests of getting the facts out in this very unusual matter, I didn't make that motion. I think you can see I had no opportunity to counsel Lieutenant Medici [MEH-dih-chee] on his Fifth Amendment rights before he tried to waive them on the stand. So under the circumstances I now move to strike that charge, and all Lieutenant Medici's [MED-ih-chee's] testimony supporting it.

LARKIN

I see your point, Commander, but I do believe that testimony was relevant to Lieutenant Medici's [MED-ih-chee's] state of mind when he did what he did in Sihanoukville [SEE-a-nook-vill] on June sixth. The testimony will stand, but I will consider the legal validity of that charge, and of Lieutenant Medici's [MED-ih-chee's] testimony and Fifth Amendment rights during my deliberations.

(*Turns to Breuner*)

Colonel Breuner, you may continue.

BREUNER

Lieutenant, let's get back to orders. You're an intelligence officer with an intelligence designator, correct?

MEDICI

No— I am an unrestricted surface line officer serving in an intelligence billet.

BREUNER

(*Puzzled*)
You don't have an intelligence designator?

MEDICI

No sir— unrestricted surface line, a ship driver— ultimately able to take command at sea, and any other operational job the Navy gives me.

BREUNER

Do you do line operations in Ha Tien [HAH-Tien]— patrols, ambushes, and the like?

MEDICI

Yes, occasionally with the Army advisors I'm stationed with, with the SEALs and our patrol boats. But my main job is intelligence collection.

BREUNER

What is your chain of command in Ha Tien [HAH-Tien]?

MEDICI

Intelligence staff and Admiral Zumwalt— a specific shore command— that's it. Unless of course there is a SOPA [SOAP-uh]— senior officer present afloat— in specific operations who will be calling the shots.

BREUNER

Is there a SOPA [SOAP-uh] in Ha Tien [HAH-Tien]?

MEDICI

I've never thought of that. The river division commander Lieutenant Gay would probably be— but I don't know if he's senior to me. When on the boats, I follow the knowledgeable boat commander's instructions— even if he's an Ensign or a third class bosunmate. He knows more about the boats than I do.

BREUNER

(*Incredulous*)
Are you saying you might be SOPA [SOAP-uh] at Ha Tien [HAH-Tien]?

MEDICI

I guess I might be— it depends on Lieutenant Gay's seniority.

BREUNER

You live with the Army Advisory Team in Ha Tien [HAH-Tien], correct?

MEDICI

Correct.

BREUNER

Does the team's senior officer— a major— give you orders?

MEDICI

No. Only about issues of our physical security on the hill— bunker, defense and evacuation drills and such. I just live there with them.

BREUNER

So you really don't take orders from anyone...

MEDICI

Intelligence staff and Admiral Zumwalt, a specific shore command. My written orders say I can come and go as I please without interference, and that I need not explain my actions to anyone. Lieutenant-Commander O'Neill didn't understand that in Sihanoukville [SEE-a-nook-vill].

BREUNER

But wasn't he SOPA [SOAP-uh] to you for operations on his own ship?

MEDICI

Yes, while on board, but I told him not to wait for me, to get underway when he was ready. To come and go in Sihanoukville [SEE-a-nook-vill], I was NOT under Lieutenant-Commander O'Neill's operational control.

BREUNER
(*Exasperated*)
Lieutenant— do you take anyone's orders in this war?

MEDICI

Intelligence staff, Admiral Zumwalt, and SOPA [SOAP-uh]— only if operations require.

BREUNER
(*With oomph and frustration*)

Lieutenant, it sounds like you think you must obey only the orders you choose— Maybe YOU'RE the cowboy in Ha Tien [HAH-Tien]!

CARLSON
Objection— badgering the witness and argumentative. Move to strike!

LARKIN
Sustained and stricken. Any more questions, Colonel?

BREUNER
(*Throws up his arms, looks through papers trying to regain his composure*)
One moment please, your honor. Lieutenant, why did you get your pistol before going to the warehouse around 1630 on June 6th?

MEDICI
Just a hunch that something was wrong down at the warehouses. I have a lot of experience being unarmed in strange places— when in doubt, I take the pistol.

BREUNER
Was the pistol loaded?

MEDICI
Yes.

BREUNER
Cocked?

MEDICI
Not till I was in the warehouse and saw what Metcalf was doing.

BREUNER
Did you aim the pistol at Metcalf?

MEDICI
Yes, I held it with both hands— I was shaking a little.

BREUNER
Was your finger on the trigger as you held the pistol aimed at Metcalf?

MEDICI

Yes— but I didn't remember pulling the trigger. He hit me in the head with the knife, then was on me like a ton of bricks. All I remember was the shock of hearing the pistol discharge...

BREUNER

Lieutenant, do you admit you shot Metcalf in the leg during the scuffle?

MEDICI

I really don't remember shooting— just the crack of the shot when he was on me...

BREUNER

(*Shakes his head*)
Nothing further, your honor.

LARKIN

Redirect, commander?

CARLSON

(*Looks cautiously at Medici, shakes his head no*)
No, your honor.

LARKIN

Any more witnesses, commander?

CARLSON

Yes, Lieutenant jaygee William C. Kelly, SEAL Team One, DET [dett] Bravo.

KELLY

(*Kelly comes in steel door.*)

YEOMAN

Do you solemnly swear that the testimony you are about to give will be the truth, the whole truth and nothing but the truth, so help you God?

KELLY

I do.

CARLSON

Please state your full name and duty station.

KELLY

Lieutenant jaygee William C. Kelly, 7-3-0-9-9-9, executive officer, SEAL Team One, DET [dett] Bravo.

CARLSON

You are qualified as a SEAL, Lieutenant?

KELLY

Yes.

CARLSON

How long have you been Executive Officer?

KELLY

Two months. I was spot promoted to the Exec job, for which I volunteered.

CARLSON

How many combat missions have you had in Vietnam?

KELLY

Two, in my first six weeks in-country.

CARLSON

And then you became Exec?

KELLY

Yes. Our Exec was MEDEVACed after being wounded on a mission earlier this year.

CARLSON

How old are you, Mr. Kelly?

KELLY

Twenty-two, sir.

CARLSON

What are your duties as Exec of DET [dett] Bravo?

KELLY

I am responsible for readiness of our DET [dett]— personnel, weapons and supplies, and mission scheduling.

CARLSON
How are missions scheduled?

KELLY
In two ways: First, directly with Admiral Zumwalt's staff through the Special Warfare Group commander. Second, by special assignments from SOG, with whom we maintain direct liaison.

CARLSON
Who is the direct liaison person from DET [dett] Bravo to SOG?

KELLY
Technically, our commanding officer, but he has delegated that duty to me.

CARLSON
So you are DET [dett] Bravo's direct contact with SOG for special assignment scheduling of SEAL personnel?

KELLY
Yes.

CARLSON
Did you direct petty officer Metcalf to destroy the warehouses at Sihanoukville [SEE-a-nook-vill] on June 6th 1970, if they contained communist weapons?

KELLY
(*Shifts weight in chair*)
I'm not at liberty to say, commander.

CARLSON
Please answer the question, Lieutenant.

KELLY
I'm not at liberty to testify regarding any SOG missions, sir.

CARLSON
(*To Larkin*)
Would the Board please direct the Lieutenant jaygee to answer?

LARKIN
Yes. Answer the question, Lieutenant jaygee Kelly.

KELLY

I am not at liberty to answer, sir.

LARKIN

Son, I will hold you in contempt of this Board if you don't answer.

KELLY

Sir, I am not at liberty to answer any questions about SOG missions—

(*Kelly pulls scrap of paper out of pocket and reads*)

Per National Security Council Directive 68-009.

CARLSON

Lieutenant jaygee Kelly, who is your contact at SOG regarding special assignment missions for DET [dett] Bravo personnel?

KELLY

I'm not at liberty to say, sir.

CARLSON

In planning Metcalf's Sihanoukville [SEE-a-nook-vill] mission, did you discuss with your contact at SOG the consequences of the mission to the new Cambodian government? Or to USS GARRISON COUNTY and its crew?

KELLY

I'm not at liberty to say, commander. Please understand that these are standing orders regarding all matters related to SOG.

LARKIN

We will take a short recess, gentlemen. Lieutenant jaygee Kelly, please remain so I can speak with you privately, and so we can call your commanding officer on the secure phone while the others are outside.

> (*All rise and leave room through steel door, except Larkin and Kelly who stand at secure red phone in corner stage right. Kelly dials*)

> (*Lights fade.*)

ACT TWO

SCENE 4

(*Lights up. Scene: same: All seated.
Kelly off witness stand.*)

LARKIN
(*Perturbed and unsettled.*)
Gentlemen, I'm afraid I must excuse Lieutenant jaygee Kelly as a witness. What he said about his orders is correct, and we would need a National Security Tribunal order to compel him to testify about his involvement in any MACSOG derived operations.

CARLSON

(*Confers intensely with Medici*)

LARKIN
Commander Carlson, any more witnesses?

CARLSON
Recall Lieutenant-Commander O'Neill.

(*O'Neill comes in steel door, takes stand.*)

Remember, commander, you are still under oath.

O'NEILL
Yes.

CARLSON
You told us earlier that you had not considered the consequences to GARRISON COUNTY and her crew if Metcalf's mission to blow the warehouses succeeded, correct?

O'NEILL
Yes. I didn't know about the mission till after Metcalf was shot.

CARLSON
Why did you order your ship's armorer, Gunnersmate second class Zont, to dismantle the explosives rigged by Metcalf in the warehouse?

O'NEILL

I didn't.

CARLSON

Who did?

O'NEILL

My acting Exec, Lieutenant jaygee Poe, exceeding his authority, I might add. Zont was one of the party Poe took to the warehouse. When they broke up the fight between Lieutenant Medici [MEH-dih-chee] and Metcalf, Poe told Zont to dismantle everything ASAP [Ay-sapp], put the warehouse back in order, and chuck everything off the pier, while they brought Metcalf and Medici [MEH-dih-chee] back to the ship.

CARLSON

Then Lieutenant jaygee Poe saved your ship, correct?

O'NEILL

That's not the way I looked at it. I gave him a letter of reprimand when I realized he had acted on his own initiative without asking me, and that Zont's dismantling assisted in disrupting Metcalf's mission.

CARLSON

(*With disbelief*)

Are you out of your mind, commander? Poe saved your ship and your crew from death or injury!

BREUNER

Objection! Argumentative!

LARKIN

Sustained.

O'NEILL

(*Looks smugly at Carlson*)

Depends how you look at it.

CARLSON

(*Shakes his head*)

Nothing further of this witness your honor.

LARKIN

Any cross, Colonel Breuner?

92

BREUNER

(*Gazes at O'Neill, contemplatively, then turns
          to Larkin*)

I don't think so, your honor.

O'NEILL

(*Leaves witness stand for his seat*)

MEDICI

(*Begins to stand*)

I have something to say, your honor.

CARLSON

(*Jumps to his feet, keeps Medici seated with hand
          on his shoulder*)

Your honor, I think my client has said quite enough.

LARKIN

Let him speak, commander. The evidence is closed.

CARLSON

(*Grabs Medici's arm, whispers loud*)

Watch yourself, mister!

MEDICI

(*Stands, faces Larkin and Metcalf from
          counsel table*)

There's something I need to say. I've found it hard to defend
my job and my conduct at Ha Tien [HAH-Tien] and Sihanoukville
[SEE-a-nook-vill]. Everything is so complicated— the war,
Rules of Engagement, Cambodia, neutrality, chain of command,
conflicting orders and missions, and their consequences. I want
the Board to know three things directly and unequivocally from
me:

First, I am a sensible and patriotic officer. My job has left
me privy to secrets and contradictions and dilemmas I never
would have chosen to explore on my own. I'm doing the best job
I can as NILO Ha Tien [HAH-Tien], in fact NILO Cambodia, at
physical risk to myself, and now it appears even legal risk
and risk of my career in the Navy. All because I tried to
do the best job I could in dealing with the dicey Cambodian
situation.

Second, I want the Board and Gunnersmate Metcalf to know how immeasurably sorry I am that he was wounded in the melee at Sihanoukville [SEE-a-nook-vill]. I have heard that his career as a SEAL is over because of it. It keeps me awake at night thinking about the fact that I harmed a fellow sailor. I'm not a killer— I'm a collection guy.

Finally— after all that said— to a CERTAINTY in my mind, the warehouses and pier at Sihanoukville [SEE-a-nook-vill] should not have been destroyed at that time because of their importance to the survival of Cambodia. I do not waiver in that assessment. Thank you.

> (*Medici sits down*)

LARKIN

Very well.

> (*Looks to Breuner and Carlson*)

If you gentlemen are ready to summarize— briefly— I can begin my deliberations this afternoon, and we'll all plan to re-convene here—

> (*Looks at his calendar, turns back to Breuner and Carlson*)

— three days hence. Summation, gentlemen?

> (*Lights fade— longer darkness, 10-15 seconds to show more elapsed time*)

ACT TWO

SCENE 5

(*Lights up. Scene: Same, three days later. Breuner, Metcalf, O'Neill, Carlson, Medici, and Yeoman standing, Larkin walks in and takes seat. All others then sit.*)

LARKIN

Gentlemen, this has been a hard inquiry and harder deliberation. We've all been exposed to aspects of this war that are classified beyond imagination, but worse, are contradictory and embarrassing, and have demonstrated the cross-purposes of our elaborate intelligence establishment, especially its covert operations. What we've seen shows us this is no way to run a railroad— but that really is for my recommendations to the Commander of Naval Forces here, to the Chiefs of Naval Operations and Intelligence, and their counterparts at MACV [MACK-vee].

I've listened carefully to the far-ranging testimony I've purposely allowed to help us all fairly grasp these matters. The principal witnesses are young, dedicated and patriotic officer and petty officer, and our Navy is proud of them both for their service.

Nonetheless, cross-purposes of our secret intelligence programs have caused serious physical injury to petty officer Metcalf, probably ending his operational career, and have called into question the methods of Lieutenant Medici [MEH-dih-chee] in his unbridled intelligence collection efforts, with the possibility of his naval career also ending, should charges be brought and proved.

I considered these matters carefully for nearly three days before deciding what to do. The linch pin of my decision is the bedrock tradition of independence of command in the United States Navy—

(*Looks at Breuner*)

and I include the Marine Corps, Colonel. As compared to the land-based services, the Navy— because its assets were far-flung and out of touch with central command much of the time— had to vest its commanders, junior officers and petty officers absolute discretion to assess the on-scene situation and act immediately, in accordance with their best judgment. This tradition began in the British navy when it covered the known world, whose admiralty could only give squadron commanders general orders, such as—

(*Reads from paper*)

"Interdict French shipping on the Spanish Main"— for a cruise that might last four years. Gentlemen, our service's tradition is— the buck stops with the on-scene commander. He has to have the big picture, know the mosaic of background details, and act boldly and quickly when confronted with unusual situations.

At Sihanoukville [SEE-a-nook-vill] on June sixth, there was a confluence of events that in my judgment could not be perfectly resolved by any man there.

Lieutenant-Commander O'Neill— a careful commanding officer— was, unfortunately, not privy to any of the background events that brought Lieutenant Medici [MEH-dih-chee] and petty officer Metcalf to Sihanoukville [SEE-a-nook-vill] with their own specific covert missions. Under the circumstances he acted very conservatively— and cannot really be faulted for it— in disliking Lieutenant Medici's [MED-ih-chee's] conduct while on board GARRISON COUNTY.

Of course, Lieutenant-Commander O'Neill knew nothing of Lieutenant Medici's [MED-ih-chee's] collection mission to seek ways to disable the port, nor petty officer Metcalf's covert mission to destroy the warehouses. Because he was uninformed about the missions or the political background of our dealings with Cambodia, he could not be considered SOPA [SOAP-uh]— Senior Officer Present Afloat— on the ground at Sihanoukville [SEE-a-nook-vill].

Sections 0929, and 0930 of Navy Regulations on SOPA [SOAP-uh] support my view, in excluding from a SOPA's [SOAP-uh's] command quote— "such units as may be assigned to shore commands by competent authority" unquote— as Lieutenant Medici [MEH-dih-chee] and petty officer Metcalf were here, on Admiral Zumwalt's and SOG's orders.

As relates to Lieutenant-Commander O'Neill ordering Lieutenant Medici [MEH-dih-chee] to stay aboard his ship, Section 0907 directs SOPA quote— "NOT to divert a command from an operation or duty assigned by another authority unless the public interest demands," unquote. 0907 leaves unresolved SOPA's authority to divert a subordinate whose orders are not to be disclosed, as both men's covert orders were here.

Properly, as commanding officer of his ship and crew, Lieutenant-Commander O'Neill gave orders he believed would protect his ship and crew, without knowledge of the two underlying missions. On that count, I conclude that his order to Lieutenant Medici [MEH-dih-chee] to remain aboard GARRISON COUNTY when he returned to the ship at 1630, in light of Lieutenant-commander O'Neill's lack of information and in light of Lieutenant Medici's [MED-ih-chee's] written freedom-of-movement and non-disclosure orders from his shore command, CANNOT be considered a lawful order to Lieutenant Medici [MEH-dih-chee], and Lieutenant Medici's [MED-ih-chee's] disobeyal of it should not result in Article 92 charges against him.

CARLSON

(*Carlson smiles and lays his hand on Medici's arm.*)

LARKIN

(*Looks directly at O'Neill*)
Also, after careful consideration, I strongly recommend that Lieutenant-Commander O'Neill reconsider his letter of reprimand to his Exec, Lieutenant jaygee Poe, and instead consider a decoration for that young officer's quick thinking, which likely saved GARRISON COUNTY and its crew, and the lives of petty officer Metcalf and Lieutenant Medici [MED-ih-chee]. I ask you, lieutenant commander, to report back to me personally within sixty days on what action you have taken on this recommendation.

(*Turns to Medici*)

Similarly, on the issue of lawful orders, Lieutenant Medici [MEH-dih-chee] CANNOT be subject to an Article 92 charge for interfering with petty officer Metcalf's unwritten and unproven mission orders. There is frankly doubt in my mind, after hearing Mr. Kelly's testimony— or lack of it— of the lawfulness of petty officer Metcalf's mission orders, from SOG or from whomever transmitted. Even if the mission were considered technically lawful, the evidence has shown it might not have been well thought out, as to impact on the fragile new Cambodian government, and as to the clear potential danger to Lieutenant-Commander O'Neill's ship and men, who were unwitting and uninformed accomplices. We'll never know, but the SOG planners may have been inadequately informed, and their mission folly.

I think Lieutenant Medici [MEH-dih-chee] thought quickly in the fog of war, evaluated his course of action rationally and intelligently, and, as SOPA on the piers in Sihanoukville [SEE-a-nook-vill], he properly ordered petty officer Metcalf to desist.

Petty officer Metcalf, a trained operative, responded second nature to the threat he perceived Lieutenant Medici [MEH-dih-chee] posed to his mission, and we cannot fault him, now or in future proceedings, for doing all in his power to complete his mission. I would remind Lieutenant Medici [MEH-dih-chee] that despite his initiative, if the men from GARRISON COUNTY had not arrived when they did, both he and petty officer Metcalf might be dead, the warehouses at Sihanoukville [SEE-a-nook-vill] destroyed, and perhaps the fragile new government fallen.

On the Article 92 charges related to the mortar ammunition you have asked me to consider against Lieutenant Medici [MEH-dih-chee], Colonel Breuner, I don't think it fair to use the Lieutenant's own testimony against him, when he admitted the facts on the stand in a flurry without proper consultation with his lawyer about his Fifth Amendment privilege against self-incrimination, and you put on no evidence of the charges in your case in chief. And frankly, in Lieutenant Medici's case, the six cases of mortar ammunition he sent to help save a loyal agent doesn't seem untoward, and in fact seems like the American thing to do.

Further, I completely reject the Judge Advocate's request for Article 104 charges of aiding the enemy— the furthest thing from the minds of these two brave young men on the pier at Sihanoukville [SEE-a-nook-vill].

(*Looks at Breuner*)

The Article 88 charges, disrespecting civilian authority— probably based on a thoughtless, salty epithet— are absurd, and no evidence was entered on them in your case in chief.

(*Sits up; turns stern face to Medici*)

However, Lieutenant, a good man has been injured and it is clear from the testimony that you have a record, in your short time as NILO Ha Tien [HAH-Tien], of pushing the gray areas to their limits, by conscious calculation. A Presidential Order, young man, is a Presidential Order, extenuating circumstances or not. You might care to remember in your naval career— if it goes further— that General MacArthur was fired by his Commander-in-Chief, Harry Truman, for just such insubordination in Korea, regardless of extenuating circumstances. The chain of command and discipline to obey orders mean something in this Navy and under our Constitution. I caution you, Lieutenant, during the rest of your tour at Ha Tien [HAH-Tien], to reflect upon the calculated rule-bending which characterized your first six months, and almost cost a fellow sailor his life. And to remind you I will draft a Letter of Caution for your service jacket, focusing on your tendency toward recklessness.

(*Looks at Breuner*)

Colonel, anything else?

BREUNER

No, your honor.

LARKIN

Commander?

CARLSON

No, your honor.

99

LARKIN

Very well, these proceedings are concluded. No charges are recommended to be filed against Lieutenant Medici [MEH-dih-chee] or petty officer Metcalf, and a letter of reprimand will be drafted by the Board for placement in Lieutenant Medici's [MED-ih-chee's] file.

(*Taps gavel, rises and leaves*)

(*Breuner helps Metcalf to his feet, stares and shakes his head at Medici; all exit except Medici and Carlson.*)

CARLSON

You happy? You beat the rap.

MEDICI

Happy? No. I'm the youngest lieutenant in the Navy. What do you think that letter of caution is going to do to my chances for promotion at the Lieutenant-Commander Selection Board, or for command?

CARLSON

(*Startled, cannot believe Medici's audacity.*)
Promotion? Command? Are you kidding, Lieutenant? You may have beat the filing of criminal charges, but you'll never have a command, I'll tell you that.

(*Pauses.*)

Do you think this is some kind of game? You did what you did, and it came to this Board's attention. You may have saved the flaky Cambodian government for awhile, but you ruined two careers, Metcalf's AND yours. At least you don't have a gunshot wound to show for it.

(*Stands up straight, salutes Medici.*)

I wish you a fair wind and a following sea, Lieutenant. At least I kept you out of Portsmouth brig!

(*Carlson turns and walks out door, upstage right.*)

100

MEDICI
(*Stands gaping at Carlson.*)
But commander, you don't understand. You can't
understand...

(*Actors freeze, all heads down, stage fades
half-dark, while overvoice recites:*)

OVERVOICE
On April 17, 1975, Pol Pot's Khmer Rouge forces captured
Phnom Penh [Nom-Pen] with weapons from the Sihanoukville
[SEE-a-nook-vill] cache, and began their Killing Fields
reign of terror in Cambodia. Lon Nol [Lahn Nole] and his
aides fled to Hawaii.

(*Curtain.*)

END OF PLAY

Printed in the United States
by Baker & Taylor Publisher Services